THE LEGEND OF
POLARIS®

THE LEGEND OF
P★LARIS®

50 YEARS

1954 • USA • 2004

JEFFREY L. RODENGEN & RICHARD F. HUBBARD

Edited by Melody Maysonet
Design and layout by Rachelle Donley and Wendy Iverson

Write Stuff Enterprises, Inc.
1001 South Andrews Avenue
Second Floor
Fort Lauderdale, FL 33316
1-800-900-Book (1-800-900-2665)
(954) 462-6657
www.writestuffbooks.com

Polaris part number: 2834921

Publisher's Cataloging in Publication

Rodengen, Jeffrey L.
    The legend of Polaris/ Jeffrey L. Rodengen. & Richard F. Hubbard: edited by Melody Maysonet; design and layout by Rachelle Donley and Wendy Iverson. — 1st ed.
    p. cm.
    Includes bibliographical references and index.
    LCCN 2002115058
    ISBN 0-945903-92-8

1. Polaris Industries — History. 2. Motor vehicle industry — United States — History. 3. Motor vehicles — Recreational use — United States — History. I. Hubbard, Richard F. II. Title.

HD9710.U54P65 2003   338.7'6292'0973
                     QBI03-200400

Library of Congress
Catalog Card Number 2002115058

ISBN 0-945903-92-8

Completely produced in the
United States of America
10 9 8 7 6 5 4 3 2 1

Also by Jeffrey L. Rodengen

The Legend of Chris-Craft

IRON FIST: The Lives
of Carl Kiekhaefer

Evinrude-Johnson and
The Legend of OMC

Serving the Silent Service:
The Legend of Electric Boat

The Legend of
Dr Pepper/Seven-Up

The Legend of Honeywell

The Legend of Briggs & Stratton

The Legend of Ingersoll-Rand

The Legend of Stanley:
150 Years of The Stanley Works

The MicroAge Way

The Legend of Halliburton

The Legend of
York International

The Legend of
Nucor Corporation

The Legend of Goodyear:
The First 100 Years

The Legend of AMP

The Legend of Cessna

The Legend of VF Corporation

The Spirit of AMD

The Legend of Rowan

New Horizons:
The Story of Ashland Inc.

The History of
American Standard

The Legend of Mercury Marine

The Legend of Federal-Mogul

Against the Odds:
Inter-Tel—The First 30 Years

The Legend of Pfizer

State of the Heart:
The Practical Guide to
Your Heart and Heart Surgery
with Larry W. Stephenson, M.D.

The Legend of
Worthington Industries

The Legend of
Trinity Industries, Inc.

The Legend of IBP, Inc.

The Legend of
Cornelius Vanderbilt Whitney

The Legend of Amdahl

The Legend of Litton Industries

The Legend of Gulfstream

The Legend of Bertram
with David A. Patten

The Legend of
Ritchie Bros. Auctioneers

The Legend of ALLTEL
with David A. Patten

The Yes, you can of
Invacare Corporation
with Anthony L. Wall

The Ship in the Balloon:
The Story of Boston Scientific
and the Development of
Less-Invasive Medicine

The Legend of
Day & Zimmermann

The Legend of Noble Drilling

Fifty Years of Innovation:
Kulicke & Soffa

Biomet—From Warsaw
to the World
with Richard F. Hubbard

NRA: An American Legend

The Heritage and Values
of RPM, Inc.

The Marmon Group:
The First Fifty Years

The Legend of Grainger

The Legend of
The Titan Corporation
with Richard F. Hubbard

The Legend of Discount Tire
with Richard F. Hubbard

The Legend of La-Z-Boy
with Richard F. Hubbard

The Legend of McCarthy
with Richard F. Hubbard

Jefferson-Pilot Financial:
A Century of Excellence
with Richard F. Hubbard

InterVoice:
Twenty Years of Innovation
with Richard F. Hubbard

TABLE OF CONTENTS

FOREWORD

BY

Hall Wendel

retired chairman, president, and CEO of Polaris Industries, Inc.

WHEN I JOINED POLARIS in 1972, it was a division of a much larger company called Textron, and it had only one main product, the snowmobile. Today, Polaris is a publicly traded, multi-billion-dollar corporation that produces a diverse line of recreational vehicles. We offer snowmobiles, all-terrain vehicles, Workmobiles™, the Polaris *RANGER,* personal watercraft, motorcycles, and, most recently, a sport boat line.

By any measuring stick, Polaris is a staggering success, but its future hasn't always been certain. Fortunately, our passion for the products we make and our dedication to making innovative products and features have seen us through the hard times. That hasn't changed since the company's founding in 1944 in the little town of Roseau, in northern Minnesota.

I was only two years old when Edgar and Allan Hetteen and David Johnson opened a machine shop called Hetteen Hoist & Derrick, the company that would soon become Polaris Industries. The founders began their business by inventing and manufacturing unique farm implements such as hoists, derricks, and sprayers. An innovative straw cutter and sprayer was

the company's most lucrative product. Then in 1955, David Johnson invented the snowmobile.

Like many people in Roseau, David loved the great outdoors. He also enjoyed tinkering and wanted to make a sort of mechanical toboggan that could travel over deep snow and take some of the work out of outdoor life. That's when he cobbled together a strange-looking snowmobile contraption later dubbed "Number One." None of the founders intended to make money from the invention, but when Polaris couldn't make its payroll one week, that's exactly what happened. A local resident who had to walk six miles in the snow to cut pulp purchased Number Two for $650.

The rest, as they say, is history. But as with many success stories, the path was fraught with snowdrifts.

Edgar Hetteen's famous, 1,200-mile snowmobile trek across Alaska in 1960 generated national interest and helped prove the snowmobile's reliability. After that, it didn't take long for competitors to muscle in for a piece of the action. Though Polaris engineers kept turning out more advanced models, the company struggled throughout the 1960s and often found itself strapped for cash. That's why the Polaris board decided to sell the company to

Textron Incorporated in 1968. By the time I joined what had become Textron's Polaris E-Z-Go division in 1972, snowmobile sales were sluggish. Two energy crises, spiraling interest rates, an influx of competitors, and consistently low snowfall in the 1970s didn't help matters. Textron was looking to get out of the snowmobile business. They named me president of Polaris E-Z-Go in 1980 and put me in charge of finding a buyer.

I couldn't find one.

So I rounded up a small group of Polaris managers who were willing to risk their life savings and go into considerable debt to buy Polaris from Textron. We completed our leveraged buyout in 1981 and ended up with a 20:1 debt-to-equity ratio. Thus began another phase in Polaris's evolution—what I call the "lean-and-mean" stage. Our livelihoods depended on being successful, and we watched every nickel. We focused on cash flow to pay down debt, to make payroll, and to put something away to grow the business in the future. Ultimately we were able to cut costs below what we had budgeted, and within two years we paid off all our debt to Textron. Within six years we had gone from being number four in the snowmobile business to being number one.

Product innovation has always been our greatest strength. Once we became number one in snowmobiles, we had the opportunity to expand into other areas. We knew we were good at engineering and mass assembly, so we set out to make products that leveraged those strengths. We created the first automatic transmission ATV in 1985, engineered the first electronically fuel injected snowmobile in 1989, introduced a stable and reliable two-seat personal watercraft in 1992, and in 1997 crafted a much lauded, custom-styled motorcycle cruiser called Victory, the first widely distributed American-made motorcycle in 60 years.

During all of its 50 years, Polaris has maintained an unwritten code: If you want to know what the customer wants, if you want to build a better product, you need to ride the product and understand the experience. We are close to the customer because we *are* the customer. All employees of Polaris are enthusiastic riders. We enjoy the sport, and you just can't replace that kind of insight.

We fostered a culture that encouraged every employee to get out and ride. For example, I encouraged the sales and marketing team at the Minneapolis headquarters to ride with the engineers and production people on the so-called Roseau Engineers Ride. I encouraged them to ride Polaris products in progress as well as competitive products. After the ride, we all got together to compare notes, and we were all open about what we liked and disliked, whether it was a Polaris product or a competitive one. Then we'd summarize what we had to do to continue bringing the best product we could to our customers.

Our ability to pull together and our can-do attitude have been another Polaris strength. After running the business on a shoestring budget during the 1980s, I look back and realize it was a blessing in disguise because running lean and mean became ingrained in us. We had clear lines of communication and responsibility, and we were forced to make decisions at the lowest possible level. We've always operated under the mantra, "If there's a better way, we'll find it," and that, also, has made us successful. Our plants are in small communities that share a hardworking Midwest work ethic, and our people take tremendous pride in what they do. They're close to the land, and they love the great outdoors. That's one of the reasons I joined Polaris. Since I was a kid, I've loved the outdoors. I've climbed mountains and run marathons, and I love to ride the products Polaris makes.

I spent my entire 30-year working career at Polaris, and though it hasn't always been easy, I haven't regretted a single moment. When it came time for me to step down as company leader, I knew I had an ethical obligation to the people who served me well to make sure they were in good hands going forward. Now that Tom Tiller is president and CEO, I'm confident that Polaris people will continue following the edicts that have made the company so successful: Understand the riding experience. Live the riding experience. Work to make it better.

ACKNOWLEDGMENTS

A GREAT NUMBER OF PEOPLE ASSISTED IN the research, preparation, and publication of *The Legend of Polaris.*

This book would not have been possible without the professional skills of our talented research assistant David Kenney. His efforts went a long way toward making this book a success. Melody Maysonet, senior editor, oversaw the text and photos from beginning to end, and Rachelle Donley's and Wendy Iverson's graphic design brought the story to vivid life.

Several key people within Polaris Industries lent their invaluable efforts to the book's completion, sharing their memories and providing valuable oversight for accuracy: Ron Bills, Mark Blackwell, Jeff Bjorkman, Edgar Hetteen, David Johnson, Mitchell Johnson, Marlys Knutson, Bennett Morgan, Robert Nygaard, Ed Skomoroh, Ken Sobaski, Scott Swenson, and Tom Tiller. In addition, Marlys Knutson helped guide the book's development from outline to final form, and Cindy Ranem was a great help in coordinating interviews.

Many other Polaris executives, employees, retirees, and friends greatly enriched the book by discussing their experiences. The authors extend particular gratitude to these men and women for their candid recollections: Chuck Baxter, Jim Bernat, Darcy Betlach, Bessie Billberg, Rudy Billberg, Ben Blackmon, Marlys Brandt, Wanda Campbell, Clayton Carlson, Gary Cooper, John Corness, Chuck Crone, Todd Dannenberg, Tim DeJong, David Dokken, Bob Eastman, Richard Edwards, Jerry Endrizzi, Bob Evans, Bill Fisher, Lloyd Fugleberg, Bob Granitz, Gary Gray, Dean Hedlund, Donald Hedlund, Greg Hedlund, Martin Heinrich, Mike Hetteen, Pam Hetteen, Joe Hovorka, Janet Klis, Paul Knochenmus, LaRae Krahn, Judy Kulsrud, Mike Malone, Robert Moe, Kevin Mollet, Dave Mona, Udell Nelson, Arlen Ness, Arnie Ochs, Marlys Olsen, Duane Osell, Richard Petty, Dick Pollick, Jerry Shank, Bruno Silikowski, Jeff Whaley, Ken Wojciehowski, and Mary Zins.

As always, special thanks are extended to the dedicated staff at Write Stuff Enterprises, Inc.: Jon VanZile, executive editor; Heather Deeley, associate editor; Bonnie Freeman and Dan Ruck, copyeditors; Sandy Cruz, senior art director; Dennis Shockley, art director; Mary Aaron, transcriptionist; Barb Koch, indexer; Bruce Borich, production manager; Marianne Roberts, vice president of administration; Sherry Hasso, bookkeeper; Linda Edell, executive assistant to Jeffrey L. Rodengen; Lars Jessen, director of worldwide marketing; Irena Xanthos, manager of sales, promotions, and advertising; Rory Schmer, distribution supervisor; and Jennifer Walter, administrative assistant.

A caravan of Sno-Travelers, led by Polaris cofounders David Johnson and Allan Hetteen, cruises up the Roseau River.

CHAPTER ONE

BIRTH OF A BUSINESS

1944 – 1956

There was just something about me. I had to go into business for myself.

—Edgar Hetteen,
cofounder of Polaris Industries

IN THE YEARS IMMEDIATELY following World War II, three young men with a knack for making and fixing machines went into business for themselves in Roseau, Minnesota, a small, rural town about 10 miles south of the province of Manitoba, Canada. The three mechanics from Minnesota's north country had no grand vision, no dreams of becoming captains of industry. But they did share a talent for innovation and a belief in their abilities. In the decades that followed, their little machine shop in Roseau would evolve into something they could never have imagined: a manufacturing phenomenon called Polaris Industries.

The history of Polaris is, in part, a story of innovation, persistence, and a little bit of luck. In that respect, it is very similar to the stories of many other successful companies. But Polaris is more than a cookie-cutter corporate success story. It is a story of a company that has persevered because it employs dedicated people who are committed to innovation and to their customers.

A One-Man Machine Shop

Edgar Hetteen's role began first.

Hetteen was a farm boy, the son of first-generation Swedish immigrants. He had grown up on the family's 80-acre homestead, south of Roseau, and spent hours each day milking cows, feeding livestock, and doing all the other chores that helped keep the farm running. It was there on the family farm that Edgar Hetteen developed a lifelong infatuation with machines. "Dad wasn't mechanical," he would later write, "and I was given free rein of the farm machinery."[1]

In 1934 Hetteen graduated from eighth grade, never to return to school. He landed a job at his uncle's new machine shop, the OK Welding Company (later called the OK Machine Company), in Roseau. At first Hetteen swept the floors and filled the wood stove, but before long he was learning the mechanic's trade and problem-solving strategies by listening to Oscar and Knute (the "O" and "K" in OK). "I was enthralled as they listened to the farmers' and lumbermen's problems and then came up with solutions," Hetteen recalled. "The education they gave me was responsible for all the things that were to follow."[2]

As the years went by, Edgar Hetteen honed his skills—first at the OK Welding Company, then at the local Chevrolet garage and the county highway department. He learned gas and electric welding, metal shaping, machining, and general problem

The Hetteen brothers and David Johnson named their company after Polaris, the North Star, to call attention to their location in the northern United States.

solving.[3] In the fall of 1944, after a short stint in the U.S. Navy, Edgar Hetteen decided it was time to try something new. He began preparing to go into business for himself. He would call his new company Hetteen Hoist & Derrick.

Edgar Hetteen planned to manufacture and market a new apparatus he had invented—a specially equipped rig that could hoist wooden electrical poles and plant them in the ground. The young man had one problem, however. He had no money and no prospects for securing a bank loan. With no other options available, he turned to the farmers he had worked for during his years at OK Welding and asked them to pay him in advance for future machine shop work. To his amazement, many of them agreed. "Those farmers, God bless them, trusted me," he recalled years later. "Maybe

An old sign for the Pine Needle Inn is on the back wall of the Hetteen Hoist & Derrick plant.

it was only $25 per farmer, but it was enough to feed my family and get the business started."[4]

Next he had to find a home for his new business. After searching the Roseau area, Hetteen settled on an old 30-foot-by-60-foot building on the edge of town. It was, in his words "a little rickety," but he thought it was perfect. It even had a colorful history. Years earlier the building had been a dance hall outside of Roseau called the Pine Needle Inn. The inn had shut down in the 1930s after a fatal shooting, and later the building had been moved into town. In late 1944, Hetteen approached the building's owner (a local Coca-Cola distributor) and offered to buy it on credit. After a short discussion, the owner agreed. Hetteen moved into what he called his own private Taj Mahal in early 1945.[5]

Hetteen needed steel to make his hoists and derricks, but he was still low on cash. Armed with nothing but his good word, he traveled south to Minneapolis to visit a steel company he had dealt with during his years at OK Welding and asked the company's credit manager to front Hetteen Hoist &

Derrick $40 worth of steel. The credit manager said no. With that rejection fresh in his mind and with nothing to lose, Hetteen approached another supplier called Paper, Calmenson & Company, located across the river in St. Paul. There he met a credit officer named Cy Brennan. Hetteen recalled what happened next.

> *"How much steel do you want?" Cy asked. He'd been joined by a fellow from the city desk. That guy bobbed his head up and down while he looked me over. I don't think he liked what he saw.*
>
> *"How about $400 worth?" I said. As long as I'd been rejected for $40 earlier in the day, why not shoot for the moon?*
>
> *Cy said only four words to the other man, but they were four wonderful words.*
>
> *"Ship it to him!" he ordered.[6]*

The meeting turned out to be one of the most profitable of Edgar Hetteen's young career.

With Cy Brennan's help, Hetteen Hoist & Derrick got the raw material it needed to begin manufacturing. The accommodating credit officer from Paper, Calmenson would continue to be one of Hetteen's most reliable vendors for years to come.

Hetteen found another important ally closer to home. Norman Flagstad owned the Coast to Coast hardware store in Roseau and had a good relationship with the young entrepreneur. One day in the store, Hetteen and Flagstad struck up a conversation about the future of Hetteen Hoist & Derrick.

Several Minnesota towns tried, without success, to lure the company away from its modest home in Roseau, but Edgar Hetteen turned down all offers. By 1954 it was clear that Hetteen Hoist & Derrick, soon to become Polaris Industries, was in Roseau to stay.

> *"How's life, Edgar?" [Norman] asked.*
>
> *"Fine," I said. "But to get my business really going, I need more equipment. There is just so little I can do right now."*
>
> *"How much would that cost?" Norman asked, leaning back on the counter.*
>
> *"About a thousand," I said.*
>
> *I still have trouble believing it, but before I left the store that day, I had a check for one thousand dollars. There was no talk of how I would pay it back, or what the schedule would be; no papers to sign, nothing.[7]*

Hetteen now had the cash, the building, the steel, and the equipment he needed to launch his company. But something was still missing. For his first few months in business, Edgar Hetteen was the company's only employee. When somebody brought in something to fix, "whether it was a toaster or a farm implement," Hetteen did the work himself. But soon the rigors of single-handedly keeping the business afloat began to wear on him. His first employees, among them Orlen Johnson and Leland Brandt, were young and eager, but they were also inexperienced. Hetteen realized that

Edgar Hetteen's invention that started it all: a mechanical hoist for putting electrical poles in place

he needed to bring in a seasoned mechanic who could supervise the shop while he managed the business. He needed a partner.[8]

A Three-Man Partnership

David Johnson was one of Edgar Hetteen's closest friends as well as a kind of brother, for Johnson's mother had died shortly after childbirth, and Johnson was raised by Hetteen's grandmother. Johnson and Hetteen got along well. They had played together as boys and had worked together as young men at the Chevrolet garage in Roseau.

In 1945, while Johnson was finishing up a tour of duty in China with the U.S. Navy, he received a letter from his old friend in Roseau. Hetteen described his plans for Hetteen Hoist & Derrick and

informed Johnson that he and Hetteen were going to be partners. ("I wasn't about to take no for an answer," Hetteen later recalled.)[9] Johnson didn't need much convincing. He began sending $11 checks to Roseau every month to help the fledgling business pay its bills and meet its payroll. After being discharged from the navy in the summer of 1946, Johnson returned to Roseau and stepped in as the shop foreman at Hetteen Hoist & Derrick.

At about the same time Hetteen and Johnson were forging their partnership, another mechanically minded Hetteen was entering the picture. Allan Hetteen, nine years younger than his brother Edgar, planned to graduate from high school, unlike Edgar and David Johnson, but he liked to work in his big brother's machine shop in his spare time.[10] He concentrated on auto repair and specialized in grinding crankshafts. Gradually he learned the ins and outs of the business. In 1948 Allan Hetteen graduated from high school and joined his brother and David Johnson as a partner in Hetteen Hoist & Derrick.

What had started as a one-man machine shop had evolved into a three-man partnership with a handful of employees. The three partners shared a love of machines, but the men were far from being carbon copies of each other. Each one possessed unique strengths that would help their company survive and thrive in the years to come.

Edgar Hetteen was the entrepreneur of the bunch, the visionary who was willing to invest considerable time and money on unproven ideas that others could hardly comprehend. "There was just something about me," he would write years later. "I had to go into business for myself."[11] This entrepreneurial spirit coupled with a strong sense of self-confidence made him an extraordinary salesman and product spokesman.

David Johnson had little interest in the money side of the business. He was first and foremost a mechanic, a man who enjoyed taking apart an engine and putting it back together. He also displayed an uncommon ability to bring out the best in his employees. He was, in the common vernacular, a people person. "I was mechanically minded and I also liked to work with people," he recalled. "I could work with people to tell them what we needed done and work with them to get the most out of the employees."[12]

As the youngest of the three partners, Allan Hetteen was just beginning to show signs of what would turn out to be one of his greatest strengths: a keen business instinct. "Allan [took] over the business end, for which he had a real knack," Edgar recalled. "He was young, but wise in the ways of cash flow and keeping things running."[13]

By 1948 the foundation had been laid for what appeared to be a viable regional enterprise. Hetteen Hoist & Derrick had leadership, a modicum of capital, and a business plan of sorts. But it wasn't long before the demands of the marketplace started tugging the company in directions its founders never envisioned.

From Sprayers to Choppers

The invention that had launched Hetteen Hoist & Derrick, Edgar Hetteen's electric-pole hoist, was not living up to Edgar's expectations. The invention did exactly what it was designed to do, but, as Edgar later said, "The public did not rush out to buy it. . . . The problem with being an entrepreneur, as we had to learn, was just because there is a need for something, that does not mean there is a market for it. We had to learn that unconventional products rarely could be introduced to the marketplace by conventional methods."[14] It didn't take long for the company to move on to other, more profitable products.

In 1948 Carl Wahlberg, who was Roseau's International Harvester dealer, approached Hetteen Hoist & Derrick with a proposition. Wahlberg was having trouble getting enough agricultural weed sprayers from his supplier. He wanted Hetteen Hoist & Derrick to build the tanks and booms needed to fashion 30 sprayers, for which he would supply the engines.

Hetteen Hoist & Derrick eagerly accepted the proposal, and the company's 12 employees went right to work. Carl Wahlberg soon had the machines

Hetteen Hoist & Derrick's eclectic product line included weed sprayers (left) and grain elevators (right).

he needed. By the spring of 1949, Hetteen Hoist & Derrick was producing eight Spraycraft weed sprayers a day and selling them through DuPont distributors in Minneapolis.[15]

The sprayers were just the beginning. By the early 1950s, the three partners were manufacturing a wide variety of new products out of materials on hand. And the products were constantly improving. "Edgar, he could look at something and tell right away where it needed to improve," said Paul Knochenmus, David Johnson's brother-in-law, who started working for Hetteen Hoist & Derrick in 1953. "He'd tell me to build something, and I'd build it, and then he'd look at it and say, 'Now do this and this and this,' and I could see right away that it was going to be twice as good as it was."[16]

Hetteen Hoist & Derrick built swing sets, garbage can stands, dual tractor wheel mounts, ladders, fertilizer spreaders, pickup boxes, grain elevators, and a host of other products. But of all the items it produced during this period, none was

as successful as the straw chopper. The company's operating capital in those days came from sales of the straw chopper. The three young entrepreneurs were painting them in the colors of four major farm implement companies and selling them through those organizations.

The idea behind the straw chopper was remarkably simple. Farmers knew they could increase yields by returning organic material such as straw to their soil. The trick was finding an efficient way to do it. Plowing didn't always work. Raking and burning were time consuming and difficult. But Hetteen Hoist & Derrick's straw chopper made soil replenishment easy. When attached to a combine, the machine cut up the straw left behind by the harvest and spread it evenly over the ground. By the spring of 1951, the company had produced 175 spreaders and had increased its workforce to 20 employees. Edgar Hetteen contacted a sales representative in Minneapolis in hopes of creating a national market for the machines. The rep suggested a new name: Polaris.[17]

Demand for the Polaris Straw Cutter and Spreader grew steadily over the next several years. In January 1954, Minneapolis-Moline became the first of several combine manufacturers to begin selling the machines through its dealers. The

The three Polaris founders, seven years before the birth of the machine that would change their lives. From left: Allan Hetteen, Edgar Hetteen, and David Johnson.

future of Hetteen Hoist & Derrick looked brighter than ever.[18]

By this time, people were beginning to take notice. Several Minnesota towns, including Erskine, Red Lake Falls, Thief River Falls, and Winona, tried to lure the company away from Roseau by offering tax breaks and real estate deals. But in April 1954, the Hetteen brothers and David Johnson ended speculation about a possible move when they accepted an offer from a group of Roseau businessmen. They agreed to keep the company in Roseau in exchange for $45,000 worth of preferred stock. The deal was, in effect, a $45,000 loan with a significant string attached. While the investors would own no part of the company, they would hold two seats on the board of directors, which, before then, consisted of only David Johnson, Allan Hetteen, and Edgar Hetteen, who served as president and chairman. Those same five men would comprise the board until Edgar left the company in June 1960.

Right: Allan Hetteen, who at one time had thought about starting a used car business, grinds the crankshaft of an automobile. Polaris performed such auto repair services to help make ends meet.

Below: Before the snowmobile business took off, the Polaris Straw Cutter and Spreader was the company's most lucrative product.

The innovators at Polaris responded to the needs of local farmers by designing and manufacturing a heavy-duty "farm box" to insert in the back of a pickup truck.

One other change occurred during this time. The company previously known as Hetteen Hoist & Derrick would now be known as Polaris Industries.[19] By naming the company after the North Star, the three partners were linking the company's name to its location in the North. As David Johnson pointed out, Polaris was the most northern company in the United States at that time because Alaska was not yet a state.

The Snow Machine

Despite several small additions that had been made to the building over the years, by late 1955 Polaris was outgrowing its home in the old Pine Needle Inn, especially because Edgar Hetteen was making plans for a major expansion. "The new space is a vital necessity if we are to continue our production and sales to national and international markets," he said.[20] The company had doubled production during the previous year and was now shipping its straw choppers to places as far away as France and South Africa. Business was good—

so good, in fact, that Edgar decided to take a much-needed vacation. He headed out to California to visit relatives, leaving David Johnson in charge.

Edgar might have stayed in Roseau if he had known what Johnson was about to do. David Johnson, like many people in Roseau, was addicted to the outdoors: to the lakes, swamps, and forests of northern Minnesota. During the winter he loved to ski and snowshoe to secluded camps where he could hunt deer and enjoy nature. But getting to those camps was not always easy. The snow in northern Minnesota sometimes drifted so deep that it was almost impossible to get through. To Johnson, the snow was both a delight and a regular source of frustration. "It was hard to get around in that deep snow," he later recalled. "I kept thinking there must be a better way of doing this. I was thinking of some kind of toboggan with the belt going down the center of it."[21]

By late 1955, Johnson was thinking seriously about building a machine that would take some of the work out of outdoor life. He had seen a brochure for a strange-looking contraption designed by a Wisconsin inventor named Carl Eliason. Eliason called his machine a motor toboggan. And that's what it was—a toboggan with an engine, an elevated seat, and a track that propelled the sled over the snow. Johnson was intrigued by Eliason's machine and was convinced that he could improve on the design. So in December 1955, while Edgar Hetteen was away in California, David Johnson pulled aside two other Polaris employees, Orlen Johnson and Paul Knochenmus, as helpers and went to work on his new invention.

Nearly 50 years later, Knochenmus still remembered the day Johnson started work on the snowmobile.

David Johnson came up to me and said we got to make a machine that goes over the snow. Pete Peterson across the street—Silver Pete we called him—done a lot of hunting in the wintertime, and he said he was getting too old to use snowshoes. David said Edgar wasn't very fond of the idea, but Edgar was going to be on vacation for three weeks. So we had three weeks to see what we could do.[22]

Johnson had to work with whatever materials he could scrounge. He started by purchasing a rope-starting nine-horsepower Briggs & Stratton engine from the local hardware store. Then he borrowed a variable-speed automatic clutch from some Polaris employees who were working on a power auger project. For the propulsion track, he took a grain elevator track, turned it over, and welded cleats onto it. He fashioned the machine's frame, platform, and hull-like front section from angle iron and sheet metal. He salvaged a Chevrolet bumper from a local junkyard and turned it into a pair of skis. When completed, the bulky machine weighed in at about 1,600 pounds.[23]

"It wasn't performing too good, but it was running," said Knochenmus. "The idea was there, and it improved pretty fast from that point on."[24]

On January 10, 1956, David Johnson's snow machine was ready for its first test run, but Johnson was not. While working on his invention, he had dropped a block of steel on his toe and fractured it. Orlen Johnson took over as test driver.

The first ride was not all that impressive. The machine was slow (it went about four miles per hour) and hard to maneuver. It didn't take long for it to get stuck in a snow bank. "We were having a little thought about whether there should be an apron in the track or not," said Knochenmus. "I thought it should, and Orlen and David didn't

think it was necessary. Anyway, there was a three-foot drift, and the machine got on top, and there it stopped. So we brought it back in and put an apron in it, and it started again."[25]

David Johnson was eager to show off his new invention, but when Edgar returned from California, he was not impressed. He couldn't understand why Johnson was putting so much time and effort into what looked like an overgrown toy when he could have been making money for the company. "Anger isn't the proper word to describe my emotions, but I certainly was miffed at my longtime friend," he recalled years later. "Why was David wasting his time like this? Our factory builds farm equipment."[26]

At first Edgar Hetteen tried to ignore Johnson's invention. But soon the machine started to grow on him.

More and more, in spite of myself, I was drawn to it. A week later, I noticed that it was no longer around; and I missed the thing.

"Hmmm," I thought. "David must have taken it home."

Polaris's innovative garbage can stand was designed to keep trash in and animals out.

Wayne Olson and his dog Sport take a ride on Number One, the first Polaris snowmobile ever made. The machine weighed about 1,600 pounds and moved across the snow at about four miles per hour.

Except he hadn't. He'd done what I thought impossible. He actually sold it. Pete Peterson, who owned a lumber yard across the street, had bought the first Polaris snowmobile.[27]

Johnson sold Number One to Pete Peterson for $465. "I told Pete that it wasn't a viable product yet," Johnson recalled. "I told him that it wasn't dependable, so he shouldn't go riding way off into the middle of the field someplace where he couldn't get back. Well, Pete didn't do that."[28]

As it turned out, Pete Peterson was the perfect buyer for that first snowmobile. By most accounts, Peterson was a fearless, though mechanically inept, driver. "Really, this was the best thing we did," David Johnson later recalled. "Pete was our first test driver. Pete would break down north of town, walk back out, and we'd have to go and fix it. This is how we tested and improved the machine."[29]

The lessons learned from the machine called Number One came in handy as Allan Hetteen and Polaris employee Albin Erickson started work on Number Two. Allan Hetteen planned to make several significant improvements on Johnson's earlier design. Among other advances, its engine would be bolted in place, its track would have belting between the cleats, and it would feature slide rails to keep the track from falling off during turns (an annoying habit of the first machine).[30] By the middle of February 1956, Allan Hetteen had finished his machine. He was proud of this snowmobile and planned to keep it for himself.

Number Two Brings Cash

Polaris was still cash-strapped, however, despite the mounting success of its straw choppers. If something didn't happen soon, the company would be unable to make its payroll. One day while Allan was out of town delivering a shipment of straw choppers, Edgar and David Johnson decided to try to turn Number Two into cash. After all, Edgar reasoned, it was made from Polaris material with Polaris labor.

They took Allan's new snowmobile up to Angle Inlet on Lake of the Woods, where they met with a local resident named Harley Jensen, who had expressed interest in the machine. Every day Jensen had to walk three miles to where he was cutting pulp on the mainland and three miles back, and he knew the snow machine could save him a lot of time.

Years later Jensen could still remember vividly what happened on his first demonstration ride.

David Johnson, Allan Hetteen, and Edgar Hetteen pose with the Polaris Straw Cutter and Spreader, the machine that, more than any other, kept them in business during Polaris's early years.

David gave me my very first ride, through the woods, down to the lake and back again. But when we came into the yard, the throttle cable froze and David couldn't stop the machine. He had to reach back and pull the spark plug wire. By that time I had slid off the machine and deposited myself in a snow drift.[31]

Despite the slapstick nature of the test run, Jensen agreed to buy the machine for about $650. When Allan Hetteen returned home, he was dismayed to discover that his beloved snowmobile had been sold without his knowledge. But he couldn't get too angry. The sale of Number Two helped Polaris Industries meet its payroll, and more importantly it demonstrated that there might actually be a market for the snow machines.

By May 1956, Polaris employed about three dozen people and reported sales of more than $400,000.[32] Straw choppers were still the company's bread and butter. Snowmobiles accounted for only a tiny fraction of Polaris revenues. "That first winter we built four sleds, then stopped," David Johnson recalled. "We had to work on other things to keep the bankers from the doors."[33] But David Johnson and the Hetteen brothers were, by this time, smitten with their snow machines and were already making plans to build more for the upcoming season. The trick would be to convince other people that the snowmobile's time had come.

In 1960, Edgar Hetteen, Erling Falk, and Rudy and Bessie Billberg embarked on a 1,200-mile trip across Alaska to prove the Polaris Sno-Travelers were rugged and reliable. Throughout their journey, the adventurers encountered children who marveled at the "sleds without dogs."

CHAPTER TWO

PLODDING THROUGH THE SNOW

1957–1960

Wherever we stop people are very inquisitive about our machines and the distances we have come. We feel certain that these motor sleds will change the travel habits of this country.

—from the diary of Edgar Hetteen,
on his 1,200-mile Alaskan journey, 1960

THE SNOW MACHINE needed a name. But coming up with one was a bit trickier than the Polaris founders thought it would be. Their first choice was "Pol-Cat"—an unfortunate moniker since "polecat" is another name for a skunk. On their second try, they came up with "Sno-Cat," but another company, called Tucker, already had a large, four-track vehicle on the market with the same name, and the Polaris partners didn't want to risk a lawsuit.[1] Finally Edgar Hetteen, Allan Hetteen, and David Johnson settled on a more workmanlike name: Sno-Traveler.

As cold weather approached in the fall of 1956, the three Polaris founders prepared a rudimentary business plan. They would build more Sno-Travelers, and they would try to create a market for them by developing a network of dealers.

"I decided that we had such a fine snowmobile, it was time to seek out dealers," Edgar Hetteen later recalled. "We'd learned from the straw chopper experience that, for the snowmobile to take off, we needed such people. We should go, I thought, to a place where they really had snow, where they really ought to welcome us."[2]

That, Edgar Hetteen figured, meant going to Alaska.

The First Dealer

There was never really any question about who would make that first Alaskan sales trip. Edgar Hetteen would go there himself. "I needed an excuse to get up there," he said. "It was my favorite place in the world outside of Roseau, and it always beckoned me."[3] He contacted Denny Dunham, an old friend in Anchorage, Alaska, and arranged to ship him one of the Polaris Sno-Travelers. The machine Hetteen had in mind was Number Four—a deluxe early version of the Sno-Traveler, complete with electric starter, headlights, horn, and cigarette lighter.

Edgar and his wife flew to Anchorage in January 1957, not knowing exactly where their journey would lead. They hooked up first with Steve Rugland, a former Polaris office manager who had moved to Anchorage. Rugland then took them to see Dunham, who had parked the newly arrived Number Four in his driveway. After borrowing a car and trailer from Dunham, the three snowmobile missionaries headed off for Fairbanks, Alaska, where they planned to meet another old friend from Roseau, Rudy Billberg,

---

Before settling on the name Sno-Traveler, the Polaris founders called their machines Sno-Cats and Pol-Cats.

who had become, in Edgar's words, a "full-fledged Alaskan." Edgar was certain that Billberg would be able to suggest possible dealers.[4]

The group's arrival in Fairbanks proved inauspicious. Edgar had decided it would be a good idea to make a grand entrance, so he unloaded the Sno-Traveler from its trailer and prepared to drive it triumphantly into town. "I thought it would make an awfully big splash," he said, "that everyone would gather around and say how wonderful the machine was, how wonderful I was, and inquire how they might purchase one."[5]

Edgar aimed his machine for a ditch filled to the brim with snow. Immediately he realized he had made a mistake, for as he pointed out years later, "The early snowmobiles traveled through snow, not on snow. The snow was different. We were in semi-arid country in a sense, and walking on the snow was like walking in a field of marbles. . . . The snow machine dove deep and stalled. There I sat, more than a little red-faced and quite discouraged."[6]

Above: Keeping warm on the Alaska trail with the help of Bessie Billberg's coffee. From left: Bessie, Rudy Billberg, Edgar Hetteen, and Erling Falk.

Opposite: Children from one of the villages along the Alaskan trail gape at the strange machine.

After digging the buried Sno-Traveler out of the ditch, Edgar and his two companions slunk "out of town like a whipped dog."[7] Finally they arrived at the home of Rudy and Bessie Billberg, about 15 miles outside of Fairbanks. The Billbergs offered words of admiration for the Sno-Traveler and words of encouragement to the would-be salespeople. They also introduced the Hetteens and Rugland to a friend of theirs, a regional airline executive named Sig Wien.

Wien was intrigued by the strange-looking machine in the Billbergs' yard. "What are you going to do with it?" he asked.

"Looking for dealers, if I can find any," Hetteen replied.

"You ought to take it to my friend Tommy Brower in Point Barrow," Wien said. "The snow is windblown up there, and the machine should be right at home."[8] In other words, the snow and weather conditions would be similar to those found in northern Minnesota.

Point Barrow was 500 miles away on Alaska's northern coast—inaccessible by car. Wien offered to fly the Hetteens and their machine there at no charge on one of his airline's DC-3s. The next day, Edgar and Mrs. Hetteen took off for the far edges of the Alaskan wilderness, along with their bulky, unproven Sno-Traveler.

Tommy Brower owned the general store in Point Barrow. He didn't say much when Edgar Hetteen introduced himself and explained why he had come so far. But when Edgar offered to take him for a test ride, Brower quickly accepted, climbed onto the back of the sled, and held on tight. The ride, as Edgar Hetteen recalled years later, did not go quite as planned.

Eventually, it came time to slow the throttle, only, it wouldn't slow. It was Harley Jensen all over again. The throttle, that annoying throttle, had iced up and, though we were on flat barren land heading to the ocean, we still had cabins to avoid. Even with a snowmobile that didn't go too fast, it was plenty fast when you couldn't shut it down. Suddenly a cabin came too close, and as I struggled with the throttle, I swerved. We weaved in and out, in and out. The demonstration was not going well. I hit the throttle and wrestled with it, and finally it closed and

STAYING AFLOAT

POLARIS WOULD PROBABLY HAVE succumbed during the late 1950s if it had had to depend solely on earnings from snowmobiles. In 1960—nearly five years after David Johnson built the first Polaris snow machine—snowmobiles still accounted for only 25 percent of the company's gross sales. The straw chopper remained by far the biggest revenue generator, bringing in more than twice as much money as the Sno-Travelers.[1]

"It was a struggle to get money to grow," said David Johnson. "We were doing whatever we could to keep the place from being locked up. We made everything from dog-proof garbage cans to furnaces and stainless steel tanks and equipment for the drying plant. If we ran out of things to keep the plant busy, we'd look for work. In those days every automobile had a trailer hitch, so we'd go to the automobile dealers and ask if we could make them 10 trailer hitches."[2]

Polaris's product line during its early years was a hodgepodge of moderately successful manufactured goods. The most popular of these products was the Polaris Portable Steam Cleaner. The company sold these machines to a variety of customers, including hospitals, supermarkets, hotels, and service stations. In 1960 the cleaners accounted for 10 percent of Polaris's gross sales.

Other products manufactured during this period included swivel wheel implement hitches, farm tractor dual wheel mounts, and Fli-Lite wheel-skis for aircraft. Polaris had purchased a one-third interest in Fli-Lite Corporation in 1958, hoping that airplane skis would become a big moneymaker for the company. But the investment didn't pan out. In a 1960 document, Polaris declared "its interest in Fli-Lite Corporation to be of small, if any, value."[3]

To keep the business afloat during the late 1950s and early 1960s, Polaris workers manufactured a variety of products other than snowmobiles and performed whatever repair jobs they could find.

the machine stopped. We found ourselves on a high drift that covered someone's cabin. What a mess.[9]

Edgar Hetteen poses on one of the machines that carried him across Alaska.

Hetteen was convinced that he had lost any chance at a sale, and when he returned with Brower to his store, he was ready for certain rejection. But Brower had other ideas.

"How much do they cost?" Brower asked.

Hetteen was dumbfounded. He had not expected this. He quoted Brower the retail price, minus a dealer discount, still unsure what Brower had in mind. Brower grabbed his checkbook.

"Who do I make this out to?" he asked.

Brower wanted to take immediate possession of the Sno-Traveler. Suspecting that Brower's check might bounce but needing the money for his return trip, Hetteen reluctantly agreed. (The check cleared.) The next morning, after testing his new machine on his own, Brower wrote Edgar another check for several more Sno-Travelers. He was confident he could sell the machines to his

neighbors in northern Alaska. Edgar Hetteen had snagged his first legitimate snowmobile dealer.

"I had found a true believer," Edgar said nearly 45 years later. "Tommy Brower didn't know me from Adam, yet he wrote me two checks. I had knocked on all the wrong doors trying to sell the snowmobile—welding shops, automotive, hardware—but they weren't the believers. I didn't quit. I couldn't quit, and finally I found a real snowmobiler."[10]

Stoking Interest

At about the same time Edgar Hetteen was signing up Tommy Brower in Alaska, his partners were traveling around northern Minnesota trying to drum up additional interest in the Sno-Traveler. On February 3, 1957, David Johnson and Allan

THE SNO-TRAVELER LINE

DURING ITS FIRST FEW YEARS OF snowmobile production, Polaris was content to call all of its snow machines Sno-Travelers. But soon the company started differentiating among models, using three different names: Ranger, Trailmaster, and Trailblazer.

The Ranger was the original model. Its power platform drove a separate nose section, and its wooden running skis stretched from the front of the nose section to the end of the power platform. A rear-mounted winch helped free the sled when it got mired in snow.

The Trailmaster was basically a Ranger with a bigger engine and a longer platform. It first appeared in 1957.

The Trailblazer, introduced in 1959, was the smallest of the three machines and was designed to be easily transported. A sales brochure claimed that the Trailblazer "can be readily disassembled by one man in 20 minutes; no special tools required—fits snugly into a Cessna 180 aircraft."[1]

David Johnson tests a Sno-Traveler, which during the late 1950s came in three models.

Hetteen showed off one of their machines at an ice-fishing tournament in Ely, Minnesota. On that same day, another Polaris employee, Mark Hoffard, demonstrated the Sno-Traveler at a similar event in Bemidji. Polaris had set the stage for both appearances by running what may have been the company's first snowmobile advertisements in local newspapers. The ads touted the Sno-Traveler as "A New and Exciting Means of Transportation," designed for "the man who lives and plays outdoors . . . the game warden . . . the conservationist . . . the sportsman or the fellow who just plain likes his winter fun."[11]

Hundreds of Minnesotans gawked at the Polaris snow machines that day. Many of them took test drives or were pulled behind the snowmobiles in big toboggans. In Ely, interest in the machine was so intense that "[Allan] Hetteen and Johnson just let it go and went fishing."[12]

Soon other Polaris sales reps were fanning out across the upper Midwest, spreading the good word about the Sno-Traveler. Steve Rugland, recently returned from Alaska, was among the busiest of the Polaris missionaries. After returning in March from a sales trip to Michigan, Rugland spent 10 days showing off the machine to intrigued spectators at an annual sportsmen's show in Minneapolis. As the writer of the new company newsletter, the *Polaris Pulse*, observed, "I'll bet Steve was a busy fellow down there answering questions on the Sno-Traveler because that is a product I'm sure anyone would be proud to show."[13]

Interest in the new machines slowly increased throughout 1957. In September the company shipped its first semi-trailer of Sno-Travelers to Alaska.[14] By the end of the year, the company was negotiating to test its snow machines with the U.S. Army and Air Force.[15] In January 1958, David Johnson, Allan Hetteen, and Steve Rugland spent a week in Jackson Hole, Wyoming, demonstrating three Polaris machines at a U.S. government winter survival school. The Sno-Travelers performed well enough to help all three men earn instructor status.[16]

But even with the Sno-Traveler's increasing visibility in Alaska and the upper Midwest, there was one potential market that Polaris had yet to spend much time courting: Canada. The company's founders decided the time had come to make a foray across the border.

Oh, Canada

By this time, Polaris had developed only one business relationship in Canada of any real significance—a potential distributorship arrangement with Yetmans Limited. Yetmans was a major distributor of power equipment in Western Canada and Northwestern Ontario. It had purchased one of the early Polaris snow machines and expressed interest in selling them. But the Polaris relationship with Yetmans had not yet produced much business.

In February 1958, a Yetmans sales representative named Gerry Thomas convinced David Johnson to take a pair of Sno-Travelers to the annual Trappers Festival in The Pas, Manitoba.[17] It would be, the two men agreed, a great opportunity to demonstrate the machines in front of an appreciative Canadian crowd.

As it turned out, the crowd at the Trappers Festival included one particularly appreciative Canadian who would contribute greatly to the Sno-Traveler's early success.

H. C. "Harry" Paul was a successful Canadian chainsaw distributor and a firm believer in the potential of powered snow travel. He had come to The Pas with his own custom-designed snow machine—a toboggan with an engine mounted inside a rotating track. Like Johnson and Thomas, he planned to stir up interest for his machine at the Trappers Festival. But unfortunately for Paul,

A Polaris-made Autoboggan attracts a crowd of admirers at the annual Trappers Festival in The Pas, Manitoba.

his "Autoboggan" had several serious design flaws. It broke down almost as soon as it arrived in The Pas.

Seeing the predicament of this potential competitor, Johnson and Thomas offered to give Paul a tow. They hooked up one of the Polaris Sno-Travelers to Paul's Autoboggan and dragged the disabled snow machine—not over a back road, as Paul requested, but through the middle of town. Onlookers couldn't help but get the message: the Sno-Traveler worked; the Autoboggan didn't. Not one to hold a grudge, Harry Paul shook off the stunt and struck up a good-natured conversation with the two Polaris emissaries.

It was the beginning of a lucrative relationship.

Paul soon learned that Polaris had an inventory of 20 or so Sno-Travelers. He offered to buy them all—cash up front—if Polaris repainted the machines prairie gold and relabeled them "Autoboggans." Polaris agreed. Paul hired Gerry Thomas away from Yetmans, and the two men hit the road, spreading the word about Polaris across Canada. "I felt the snowmobile had a future," Paul remarked years later. "I just knew that someday it would be a great recreation."[18]

But Harry Paul was not just a salesman with a true believer's mentality; he was also an established businessman who wasn't afraid to gamble. Over the years, his open-checkbook policy would bail out the perpetually cash-strapped Polaris more than once. "We would call Harry and say, 'We need $20,000 for payroll; can you help us out?'" recalled David Johnson. "He paid in advance for snowmobiles we would build for him."[19]

By December 1958, Harry Paul's distributorship was firmly established. The Roseau plant was churning out four or five snowmobiles a day and sending regular shipments of prairie gold Autoboggans to Winnipeg, Canada.[20] Polaris's efforts to build a distribution and dealership network were beginning to pay off.

But the Sno-Traveler still faced plenty of obstacles. The machine did not perform well on certain terrains, such as the mountains of New England. "I don't believe we have any business in trying very hard to sell these in either Vermont or New Hampshire as the mountains are entirely too steep," wrote Allan Hetteen during an East Coast sales trip.[21] Sales were improving, but Sno-Travelers still

accounted for less than one-fifth of the company's half a million dollars in gross annual sales.[22]

Most ominously, potential customers remained skeptical about the whole snowmobile concept. They weren't sure that the machines would hold up under harsh winter conditions, and many found it hard to fathom the appeal of plowing through the snow on loud, lumbering contraptions. Edgar Hetteen knew what had to be done.

Yes, there was a long row to hoe between our own convictions and being able to establish a market. It became obvious that we needed to stir the imagination. We needed to draw out the adventurers. We needed people to understand the joys of winter. Bouncing around hour after hour in that beautiful expansive wilderness, your mind goes blank. It's an escape. You can forget for a few moments that the note is coming due at the bank. We needed people to know that. We needed to prove our snow machines worked.[23]

Once again, as he had three years earlier, Edgar Hetteen decided to take a gamble on Alaska.

1,200 Miles

In November 1959, Edgar Hetteen's friends from Alaska, Rudy and Bessie Billberg, traveled to Roseau for a visit. During their stay, Rudy made a proposal to his host.

"Edgar, I've been thinking about something," he said.

"Yeah?"

"You like Alaska."

"You know I do."

"You've been wanting to test those snow machines?"

"That's right."

"What if we took a trip on those machines from around the Bering Sea Coast up into the interior of Alaska and then finished in Fairbanks?"[24]

Edgar Hetteen didn't think much of the idea at first, but the more he considered it, the more it appealed to him. "If we really could make the trip," he thought, "it would prove to the world that we were not some rag-tag company building a goofy machine. It could move us ahead by years."[25] Edgar Hetteen and Rudy Billberg started making plans.

About four months later, on March 4, 1960, Edgar Hetteen, Rudy Billberg, Bessie Billberg, and a Polaris production specialist named Erling Falk set out from Bethel, Alaska, on a 1,200-mile proving trek across the Alaskan wilderness. This was a daring feat, for as Paul Knochenmus pointed out, one of the snow machine's earliest problems was dependability. Even on short trips, he said, "You always carried extra sparkplugs with you. And it was a problem to get belts to hold up. You always carried at least two or three belts with you."[26]

"The belts would shatter when it got colder," said Edgar. "We'd take them off and take them to bed so that they were warm."[27]

The four adventurers had decided to trust their lives to three Polaris Sno-Travelers—a pair of 10-horsepower Rangers and a single seven-horsepower Trailblazer. (During the 1950s, the Sno-Traveler came in three basic models: the Ranger was Polaris's "bread and butter machine," the Trailblazer was a smaller and lighter version of

the Ranger, and the Trailmaster was a larger, longer machine with a more powerful Onan engine.) Each of the Rangers pulled a freight toboggan loaded with hundreds of pounds of food, fuel, weapons, and camping gear. The men drove the machines. Bessie Billberg rode, usually standing up, on one of the toboggans.

When Rudy and Edgar first began making plans for the trip, they didn't anticipate that Bessie would want to come along, but as she pointed out, "Edgar couldn't cook, and I didn't think Erling Falk could, and I knew Rudy couldn't, so I thought, 'Who is going to do the cooking on this trip?' Well, that was me, of course."[28]

"When she said she wanted to come along, we said absolutely not," her husband recalled

Edgar Hetteen, Erling Falk, Bessie Billberg, and Rudy Billberg pose for one last photo before heading out from Bethel, Alaska.

more than 40 years later. "That's when I found out that I wasn't the boss. Now we've been married 63 years, and I'm still not the boss."[29]

The first two days of the journey went about as well as Hetteen and his friends could have hoped. On the evening of March 5, they arrived in a village called Kalskag, about 100 miles from Bethel. "When the children of Kalskag first sighted our party," Hetteen recorded in his diary that night, "they ran to their teachers and excitedly told them that 'two sleds without dogs' were coming up the river."[30] The four snowmobilers spent the night at the home of a young couple in Kalskag. It was one of the last comfortable nights they would enjoy during the trip.

On March 6, the going started getting tough. A 48-mile portage to the Yukon River took the expedition over deep drifts, through thick forests, and across wind-scoured tundra. The four weary travelers rested for the night in a dingy old trapper's cabin.

The Sno-Traveler machines that conquered Alaska were displayed on the streets of Fairbanks (top) for everyone to see. When loaded with gear (above), they resembled nothing so much as mechanical pack mules.

Still, the Sno-Travelers were operating nearly flawlessly.

Then the expedition's luck really began to change. On March 7, the Trailblazer blew a gasket, forcing the entire crew to backtrack to a nearby village for repairs. Two days later, after covering 54 miles in a fierce wind, the four friends came across an abandoned cabin that, at first, looked to be the perfect refuge. But as Bessie Billberg noted in her diary, it didn't live up to expectations:

Spent the night in a trapper's cabin that hadn't been used for three years except by the martens. There was a lot of dried fish stored there and the animals had made the cabin filthy. We scraped and swept it all out, threw out all the fish and other filth and stayed in it! The smell was indescribable, but it was nice to get in.[31]

Over the next 17 days, Edgar Hetteen, Erling Falk, and Rudy and Bessie Billberg overcame a series of potentially catastrophic mechanical problems. The Trailblazer fell into a patch of overflow ice (a pool of river water hidden by newly fallen snow), and the friends spent two hours chipping ice away from the machine's frozen track. Then a coil failed on Erling Falk's machine. Hetteen's Ranger burned out an intake valve. But in each case, the gifted mechanics of the Sno-Traveler caravan managed to keep the machines running.

On the evening of March 24, after three hard weeks on the trail, the four adventurers arrived in Fairbanks exhausted and elated. Fairbanks Mayor Jack Wilbur greeted them and escorted them to a reception at the local chamber of commerce.

It didn't take long for Edgar Hetteen and his cohorts to discover that they had become celebrities of sorts during their three-week adventure. Kohler, the company that had manufactured the Sno-Travelers' engines, had thrown its public relations muscle behind the expedition, and its efforts had generated national interest. Newspapers and magazines from around the country were carrying stories about the trip. In the days following his arrival in Fairbanks, Hetteen described the journey in detail to a succession of reporters, making sure to put the best possible spin on the story. "Our trip was a complete success," he said. "Our mechanical problems were so minor we can call them negligible."[32]

After four years of struggle, it appeared that the Polaris snowmobile was on the verge of a breakthrough. The Alaska trek had proved the Sno-Traveler's mettle and had generated considerable publicity. The Canadian market was beginning to open up, thanks to Harry Paul's efforts. (He had sold 164 Autoboggans by January 1960.) The U.S. Navy was using a Sno-Traveler on an expedition to the South Pole. And plans were in the works for a major expansion of the company's Roseau plant. "We are about at the limit of production with our present facilities," Edgar Hetteen explained.[33] The future of Polaris was indeed looking bright.

But despite all the good signs, trouble was brewing. The spring of 1960 would turn out to be a time of upheaval at Polaris. One of the company's three founders was about to leave in a huff.

During the 1960s, Polaris began targeting a whole new demographic by featuring women in its marketing campaigns.

CHAPTER THREE

MANAGING THE DRIFTS

1960 – 1964

By 1960 it was apparent to Allan and other veterans at Polaris that there would be competition.

—Jerry Bassett, author of *Polaris Pioneers: A Star Is Born*

EDGAR HETTEEN WAS FED UP. He had returned to Minnesota from Alaska anticipating that he would be greeted as a kind of conquering hero—an intrepid adventurer who had braved life-threatening conditions to prove the worth of an unproven product. But he soon discovered that very little had changed in Roseau during the time he was away in Alaska. Plenty of people in town still snickered behind his back about his silly snow machine. A few even laughed in his face. Among the snowmobile's most vocal critics were the two outside members of the company's board of directors.

The board had been a constant irritant to Edgar Hetteen since 1954, when he agreed to take on two local businessmen as directors in exchange for what was essentially a $45,000 loan. The outsiders on the board had never really liked the snowmobile. They preferred straw choppers. "When they saw me testing the machines, kicking up snow and making noise, they cringed and seemed ashamed," Hetteen recalled. "They wanted me in a suit, sitting at my desk, making calls, selling choppers, being respectable."[1]

The trip across Alaska had not changed the board members' minds. If anything, it had hardened them against the Sno-Travelers. Edgar

Hetteen had spent about $3,000 on the journey, and the board members did not consider it money well spent.

Edgar Hetteen was clearly on a collision course with some of the Polaris directors. "When I realized that the trip had done nothing to change the board's position," Hetteen later wrote, "I decided to take the initiative."[2]

He decided to show them that they were wrong.

The Last Straw

While two of the five men on the Polaris board were not impressed with Edgar Hetteen's accomplishments in Alaska, other businessmen were. In the weeks following the Alaska expedition, several companies contacted Edgar Hetteen about purchasing all or part of Polaris. In early May of 1960, Hetteen traveled to Minneapolis to meet with representatives of three of those companies and to find out how interested they really were.

Polaris's first all-terrain vehicle, the Trail Tractor, debuted in 1963. It was a two-wheel trail bike powered by a six-horsepower single-cylinder engine.

As it turned out, they were very interested. One of them—a farm implement manufacturer named Superior Separator—went so far as to draw up a preliminary sales agreement, offering to buy Polaris's existing snowmobile inventory and to pay royalties on future sales in exchange for all rights to the Sno-Traveler. Polaris would wind up with about $300,000 in operating cash.[3]

"Here was proof," Hetteen later recalled, "that all of our research and development and expense had been worth it."[4]

Once back in Roseau, Edgar Hetteen called a special board meeting. With the board members gathered in a semicircle around his office desk, he opened his briefcase and pulled out the offer sheet from Superior Separator. His presentation to the board was brief.

You've always said this machine we've monkeyed with has no value, criticized my trip to Alaska and my promotional work, criticized it all. . . . But take a look. Here is what people will pay for that stupid machine, the one we could never capitalize, the one we could never support, the one that caused all the problems. You can have all this money and the company just the way you want it.

His point made, Hetteen then made a surprise announcement. "Do whatever," he said, "but come June 1, I will be gone."[5]

More than 40 years later, Hetteen explained his reasoning behind the decision to leave the company he had created.

By then I had put in more than 15 years of hard work and sleepless nights and lost holidays. There had been many times while on my way to work when I worried that the sheriff had locked up the place and then felt almost sorry that he had not.

If the troops had all been marching together, I would have been able to continue, but I can't argue with [the board] and give my best to the company.

I had good jobs in Roseau, but I gave them up to go out on my own. That letter in my pocket with the offer to buy the company was the key to starting over. Someone else could now answer the phone and worry about all the problems.[6]

Edgar Hetteen let the news that he was quitting sink in. He had proven to his critics on the board that the snowmobile did have value after all. Now, as he saw it, he was walking away vindicated—a free man who would no longer have to answer to people incapable of comprehending his vision. "I guess in the back of their minds, they didn't think I was serious," he later recalled, "but of course I was dead serious."[7] The board reluctantly accepted Edgar Hetteen's resignation and named Allan Hetteen acting president. The offer sheet from Superior Separator was shelved.

In early June of 1960, Edgar Hetteen and his family packed up a travel trailer and set off for Alaska, where Edgar planned to launch a new career as an independent sales representative. "My point was proven, and I left satisfied," he said. "David and Allan would now have to deal with the board."[8]

Less than a year after moving to Alaska, however, Edgar returned to Minnesota and started a new business, Arctic Enterprises, which would become one of Polaris's main competitors.

A New Era

At a meeting in Roseau on June 30, 1960, Polaris shareholders approved a plan to reorganize the company and raise new capital through a private stock offering. Allan Hetteen officially took over as Polaris's new president and general manager. David Johnson assumed the title of vice president in charge of production.[9]

Johnson was the right man for the job. He excelled in his position, not by wielding an iron fist, but by encouraging devotion among employees.

"David was an excellent guy," said longtime employee Lloyd Fugleberg. "He was very laid back, and whatever he said, he did."[10]

"He was firm enough to gain respect, and yet he had a heart of gold," said Marlys Brandt, a Polaris purchasing agent who in 1964 was the first woman hired by the company. "Everyone wanted to work hard for him."[11]

"David was always there guiding you," observed Bob Granitz, who began working at Polaris in 1963, "and if he had to suggest something, he always did it gently."[12]

EDGAR HETTEEN'S OTHER BIG ADVENTURE

EDGAR HETTEEN'S DECISION TO LEAVE Polaris put in motion a series of events that helped define the future of Polaris and the entire snowmobile industry. After spending about a year in Alaska, Edgar Hetteen returned to Minnesota determined to put his entrepreneurial skills to good use. In 1961, he landed in the town of Thief River Falls, about 70 miles southwest of Roseau. There he started a new company, called Polar Manufacturing. At first the company produced steam cleaners and Bug-O-Vac insect traps, but within a year it started making snowmobiles. Hetteen renamed his company Arctic Enterprises and christened his snow machine Arctic Cat.

Over the next several years, an intense rivalry developed between Allan Hetteen's Polaris and Edgar Hetteen's Arctic Cat. It was, recalled Edgar, a kind of sibling rivalry. "Allan and I had a very good relationship. We had the same mother, and we broke bread with her at Christmas, Easter, New Year's and at any other holiday that brought us together," Edgar later wrote. "We were good friends and good brothers. But the very next day, if I could take a deal away from him, I did, and if he could take a deal away from me, he did. If I could build a better snowmobile, I would get more of the market. If he could make a better one, then he would sell more. Consequently, we had a friendly war. And as a result, both companies benefited by getting better and better."[1]

The decision to name Allan Hetteen president was something of a gamble. He was 31 years old, and some board members wondered whether he was experienced enough to lead Polaris into what they hoped would be a period of expansion and increasing profits.[13] All the same, he seemed to be the logical choice. No one at Polaris—except perhaps David Johnson (who said he had no desire to run the company)—knew more or cared more about the company. Despite its misgivings, the board put Polaris in the younger Hetteen's hands.

The new boss wasted no time setting a new course. In his first few months at the helm, Allan Hetteen began turning Polaris Industries into what was unmistakably a snowmobile company. As far as he was concerned, most of the company's other products could never approach the snowmobile's potential. By the spring of 1961, the straw chopper—for years Polaris's cash cow—was losing its popularity and accounted for just 38 percent of the company's sales. Other products, such as Fli-Lite airplane skis, were eliminated altogether.[14]

At the same time, the company began expanding its snowmobile line. It introduced a new generation of Sno-Travelers that were smaller, lighter, and easier to maneuver than the full-size Trailmasters. They were designed for a new and undeveloped market: winter recreation users. Brochures for the new machines showed smiling—and apparently warm—men and women engaging in a variety of winter outdoor activities, including hunting, fishing, sledding, and skiing. By the spring of 1962, Sno-Traveler sales were approaching $800,000 a year, more than 85 percent of Polaris's annual revenues.[15]

Distributors and dealers were clamoring for more machines. "I hope you can produce as many as we hope we can sell," said one Minneapolis distributor.[16]

With the rapid expansion of the snowmobile line, the manufacturing plant in Roseau was bursting at the seams. The old Pine Needle Inn, expansions and all, could no longer accommodate the needs of a company that employed about 50 people and produced 14 different snowmobile models.[17] A new factory, whose planning began

Opposite: Polaris steadily built up its network of distributors (bottom) during the early 1960s, thanks in part to Allan Hetteen's efforts to explain what Polaris snowmobiles could do (upper left and upper right).

Opposite center: David Johnson, meanwhile, did more field tests for Polaris products. Here in the swamps outside Roseau, he tests a Sno-Traveler fitted with a wheel kit. *(Photo courtesy David Johnson)*

Below: David Johnson (left) oversees production during the company's first year in its new, 41,000-square-foot manufacturing plant.

on Edgar Hetteen's watch, became an urgent priority under Allan Hetteen.

Hetteen and David Johnson invited a local business leader named Robert Foley to the Polaris plant to discuss financing for a new production facility. They showed him how cramped the building already was and explained how hard it would be to expand production without a new structure. Johnson assured Foley that potential investors had nothing to fear.

"You get us a building," he said, "and we will see that it is paid for."[18]

In the summer of 1962, Foley helped organize the Roseau Research and Development Corporation (RRDC) to help Polaris solve its financing problems. The RRDC raised $40,000 and secured a $170,000 loan from the Small Business Administration for a new building on the south side of town. Under the financing plan, Polaris agreed to lease the structure from the RRDC and to assume ownership after about 20 years.[19]

Construction on the new building began in October 1962. Seven months later, in May 1963, Polaris moved into its new, 41,000-square-foot manufacturing plant. "Now we can take our distributors from any place in the world into our factory and we know they'll be impressed," said Allan Hetteen. "Before, we were ashamed to invite them in because we knew our crowded shop and facilities would be a letdown."[20]

Bob Eastman, who began working as a welder at Polaris in the fall of 1960 and quickly moved into R&D, remembered the transition to the new factory. "At the other shop, we kind of worked where we could," he said, "but at the new place, we had a real assembly line right off the bat. It looked

nice, and we were busy, too. We had a lot of orders. We hadn't been there too long before we were running two shifts."[21]

It appeared that the Allan Hetteen era was going to turn out to be an era of success and expansion. The company was building a new product, a two-wheel motorbike called the Trail Tractor, in its new building. It had just acquired the rights to a new, propeller-driven windsled, which it planned to market under the Polaris name. Snowmobile sales now topped $1 million a year. "We feel that all in all the future is rosy," Hetteen told the local newspaper. "We feel that we can continue to move ahead."[22]

But Polaris's future—at least its near future—wasn't as rosy as Allan Hetteen imagined. The snowmobile industry, which Polaris had almost single-handedly created, was becoming increasingly competitive. And in its drive to compete, Polaris was about to make a mistake that threatened its very existence.

Roots of Competition

Competition had always been in the backs of the minds of Polaris's snowmobile pioneers, but it had never been a major concern. Polaris had developed the snowmobile in what was essentially a competitive vacuum during the mid-1950s. David Johnson had easily dispatched the Sno-Traveler's first real challenger—Harry Paul's Autoboggan—at the Trappers Festival in The Pas, Manitoba, in 1958. But in 1959, another Canadian, Joseph-Armand Bombardier, had introduced a new snow machine he called the Ski-Dog. Soon renamed Ski-Doo,

it was smaller and less powerful than the Sno-Traveler, but it featured one significant innovation that Polaris had not adopted: Its engine was mounted in the front, not the back.

David Johnson first encountered the Ski-Doo during one of his return visits to the Trappers Festival. The encounter had led, almost inevitably, to a race—apparently the first company-versus-company competition on record—which the more powerful Sno-Traveler easily won. In the years that followed, Johnson continued to race, losing only when he gave his competitors a half-lap head start. "Now I suppose they'll advertise that they beat all other machines," Johnson said.[23]

But despite his easy victories at The Pas, Johnson knew that the Ski-Doo was a formidable competitor. "They had a good machine. They had

---

Above: Polaris's short-lived, propeller-driven windsled, called the Air Sled, accounted for just $15,000 in sales during the 1963–1964 season.

Below: David Johnson's dog Duchess demonstrates the easy handling of Polaris's first all-terrain vehicle, the Trail Tractor.

ALL FOR ONE

SINCE THE EARLIEST DAYS OF THE BUSI-ness, the Polaris partners fostered a distinctive company culture based on the same work ethic and family values that made the little town of Roseau so appealing. As David Johnson observed at the company's 35th anniversary, "It takes commitment and concern for your fellow man when you are working together. If you're a disgruntled worker on the floor, you're not going to make the best product.... We want that caring about the employee to carry through to the customer, to the products."[1]

"The people have made Polaris what it is," said Jerry Endrizzi, production support supervisor for the ATV division. "It's the people who have kept this company going."[2]

On more than one occasion, Polaris was so strapped for cash that it struggled to meet payroll. "That wasn't a deterrent to our people," said David Johnson. "They'd come in the office and say, 'I need some money to buy some groceries.' So we'd go into the till and say, 'Would $10 help?' We'd divide what money we had among them until we could get money for payroll, and they were just as happy. They were part of the company."[3]

Johnson remembered one year when he and Edgar Hetteen were able to show their appreciation to employees during the holiday season, despite the fact that Polaris was broke.

It was Christmas Eve, and we didn't have any money, but we were able to charge some gasoline to put in the airplane. We bought some candy on credit, then went back to the plant and filled bags with a mix of candy. Edgar was flying, and I sat in the back seat. We flew out to where Floyd Lokken, who worked in the plant, lived. We circled low, and Floyd came running out of the house. I could see his buckle-over shoes wide open, snow up to his knees as we dropped candy out of the airplane. Then we went to different plant workers' houses and dropped candy bags. The people just loved it.[4]

From the beginning, the company's employees shared a strong sense of community. They pulled together when the going got rough and were not afraid of hard work. "Polaris treated us well," said Paul Knochenmus, who left the company in 1958 to begin a long stint as the Roseau County sheriff. "In 1966, when it snowed 33 inches in three days, Polaris provided snowmobiles for the hospital. I brought one lady in on a toboggan pulled behind a snowmobile from 10 miles south of here to have a baby at the hospital."[5]

Employees themselves developed their own traditions that fostered a spirit of creativity and fun—all while maintaining a devoted work ethic.

"All of us in engineering have the opportunity to expand," said Bob Granitz, design supervisor of the Snowmobile division. "It's even documented. We're to spend a certain percentage of our time to think up new ideas, and that allows everybody the freedom to do their own thing."[6]

New employees found themselves stepping into an atmosphere of camaraderie. "There was always some kind of initiation they had to go through," said Lloyd Fugleberg, Polaris's master scheduler, who began working for the company in 1963. "People used to carry those metal lunch buckets to work. They'd set them on the table, and somebody would weld the cover shut or weld the bucket to the table. Or we'd send them all over the shop in search of a metal stretcher, going from one person to the next, and each time they'd be sent somewhere else."[7]

Though initiation for new employees may have involved some amount of teasing, the veterans were eager to help the newbies learn the ropes. "When I came here [in 1963], I was a kid," said Bob Granitz. "Everybody was so helpful, so willing to show me things, yet they would listen to me, to my ideas. We were all together, and everybody was treated the same way."[8]

us beat. They were very much lighter," he said years later. "Motor in front; ours was motor in the back and more clumsy."[24] By 1963 Johnson and Allan Hetteen could tell that Bombardier's Ski-Doo posed a serious threat. Polaris had to respond.

As Johnson put it, "Seeing the [Ski-Doo] made us think of putting the engine in the front."[25]

The Comet Crisis

In the spring of 1963, Allan Hetteen and a Polaris engineer named David Pearson flew to a glacier on Alaska's Mount McKinley to test a prototype of a new, front-engined snowmobile called the Comet. The Comet was the most user-friendly snowmobile Polaris had yet built. The two-person model could reach speeds of 25 miles an hour and climb slopes of 45 degrees. The alternator on its Kohler engine powered a center-mounted headlight. The squared-off front chassis had room for a storage compartment. Its windshield even folded down to help it fit through tight spaces.[26]

The Comet prototype performed beyond expectations, despite less-than-ideal conditions. (A storm trapped Hetteen and Pearson on the glacier for several days beyond their scheduled pickup date.) Polaris, it seemed, had developed the breakthrough machine it needed to compete with other front-engined snowmobiles such as the Ski-Doo.

Early in the 1963–64 snowmobile season, Polaris learned an ugly truth about the Comet. The machine that had performed so well on Mount McKinley performed miserably almost everywhere else. The ignitions on the Comet's Kohler engines were faulty. Its Borg-Warner clutches couldn't handle the engine's power. And the new rubber track, which seemed to work perfectly on hard glacial surfaces, got bogged down in loose snow. As David Johnson quipped years later, "There were only three things wrong with it: we had an engine that wouldn't run; a clutch and vee-belt that wouldn't stand up; and a track that wouldn't go in the snow."[27]

Distributors, dealers, and customers started returning the Comets to Roseau in droves. "We made 400 machines and got 500 back," Johnson joked.[28] Polaris fixed some of the returned Comets and wrote off the rest as losses. In

In the spring of 1963, Allan Hetteen and Polaris engineer David Pearson (inset) set up camp on Mount McKinley to test a prototype of the Comet. The tests went smoothly, but the Comet's actual performance proved dismal.

December 1963, the company halted production of the snakebit machines and started a mad scramble to avoid bankruptcy.[29]

Allan Hetteen and David Johnson contacted all of Polaris's major suppliers and described the company's situation in stark terms. If Polaris's creditors insisted on immediate payment, they explained, Polaris would go bankrupt and its vendors would get nothing. The company could recover quickly, they said, if it could put off paying its debts. Polaris was working on a new snowmobile that would revolutionize the industry, they claimed. It just needed a little more time.

Hetteen and Johnson's efforts to hold off bankruptcy soon paid off. Most of the Polaris creditors decided that it was in their best interest to help the troubled Roseau company turn itself around. A new stock offering and a new loan from the Small Business Administration promised to generate about $100,000 in working capital.[30] The company's two remaining founders had apparently bought themselves the time they needed.

Allan's son Mike Hetteen, who later became purchasing manager for engines, explained how important integrity was to his father.

If my dad said he was going to do something, he did it. After Polaris nearly went bankrupt, one of our biggest suppliers [Paper, Calmenson, which supplied Edgar Hetteen's fledgling company with its first shipment of steel] billed us for $500,000 one month, and Dad made a payment of $50 that month. He never said how much he'd pay, but he'd make a payment every month. He kept his word, and the suppliers had faith in him. He was able to keep the bankers working with him, and he worked through the Comet crisis when the company really should have filed for bankruptcy.[31]

A storm blew over the Mount McKinley glacier while Hetteen and Pearson were testing the Comet, stranding them for several days.

Despite cooperation from bankers and suppliers, by the spring of 1964 Polaris still teetered precariously. It had recorded a net loss of more than $36,000 during the previous year, due in large part to the costs of plant relocation. It had about $350,000 tied up in raw material inventory thanks to the Comet production shutdown. And according to an independent audit, it had just $270 in cash on hand.[32]

Bob Granitz, design supervisor for the Snowmobile division, remembered how uncertain Polaris's future—and his own—looked. "David [Johnson] walked up to me and gave me a hug and said, 'Bob, do you think you can wait a week or two weeks for a paycheck? We're short this week.' I told David, 'Well, don't worry about it.' And I think that's what everybody else would have told him."[33]

Though employees like Granitz showed extraordinary devotion to Polaris and no doubt contributed to its survival, the company was in dire need of a product that would breathe new life into its ailing operations. The new snowmobile it was working on would either make the company or break it.

In the early days of snowmobile racing, sled dogs sometimes provided the competition.

CHAPTER FOUR

A Booming Industry

1964–1968

*[The Mustang] really kicked off snowmobiling as we know it today.
All of a sudden we had a machine that made winter fun.*

—Allan Hetteen, early 1960s

ONE DAY IN EARLY 1964, ALLAN Hetteen called an old friend named Carl Wahlberg into his office. Wahlberg was, like Hetteen, an avid outdoorsman and a native of northern Minnesota. He had helped the Hetteens and David Johnson secure financing during Polaris's early years and had established the company's first distributorship in the western United States. Now Wahlberg was back in Roseau, and Allan Hetteen needed his help. Hetteen asked Wahlberg to try out the company's new, post-Comet snowmobile and let him know what he thought. Wahlberg agreed.

The new machine was called the Mustang. Polaris employees Vernon Johnson, Albin Erickson, and Bob Eastman had worked on the prototype throughout the winter, hoping that the effort would make people forget about the ill-fated Comet and its problems. Wahlberg took the machine to British Columbia and put it through its paces. He came away impressed. "I told Allan the Mustang was going to work," he later recalled.[1]

Wahlberg was so impressed with the Mustang that he invested "everything I had" in the company. He and Hetteen convinced suppliers to sell Polaris the parts it needed to manufacture the new snowmobiles, even though the company still owed money on the failed Comets. Production geared up.

Polaris got ready to unveil what it hoped would be its savior machine.

On June 25, 1964, about 150 Polaris dealers and distributors gathered in Roseau to get their first peek at the company's new line of snowmobiles—including the Mustang. At first they were skeptical; after all, they were the ones who had dealt directly with unhappy Comet customers during the previous winter. But after two days of conferences, classes, and demonstrations, the dealers and distributors left Roseau feeling reassured. The new Polaris snowmobile line looked great. The company insisted that it had rigorously tested its new machines to avoid any Comet-like surprises. And it promised to back up its new product line with a sophisticated dealer support program and a national advertising campaign. "We met with a lot of enthusiasm," Allan Hetteen told the local newspaper, "and I feel we have our best line ever."[2]

Snowmobile racer Jim Bernat, who started working in Polaris's paint department in 1963 and later became snowmobile engineering quality manager, remembered how Polaris so decisively changed gears for production of the Mustang.

Allan Hetteen spent much of his time during the 1960s building up the Polaris dealership network.

"We'd built thousands of Comets," he said. "Then when we came up with the Mustang, we'd haul a load of Mustangs out and haul a load of Comets in behind the plant. We had a big drag line with a weight on it, and we'd pull the engine out of the Comet and crush the bodies and put them on a railroad car."[3]

In the aftermath of the Comet catastrophe, most Polaris employees were able to see the silver lining. "The whole experience strengthened us, made us smarter," said Donald Hedlund, who started as a welder with Polaris in 1959 and retired in 1974. "We all pulled together as a result of it."[4]

Mustang Market

The Mustang was unquestionably the star of Polaris's 1965 model year lineup. The new machine came with five power-plant choices (from six to 14 horsepower) and could reach speeds of up to 35 miles per hour. It had a fully molded rubber track, leaf spring front suspension, and a new clutch that Polaris designed and built itself. ("The clutch we designed proved highly superior to all those we previously used," Allan Hetteen explained in a not-so-subtle dig at the Comet's defective Borg-Warner clutch.[5]) Even more so than the Comet, the Mustang was designed to be a recreational sled with a stable vee-type front, standard luggage compartment, and optional reverse transmission. "All of a sudden we had a machine that made winter fun," Hetteen said.[6]

Polaris launched the biggest marketing campaign in its history to support the new machine. It formed a special team to help distributors and dealers put on field tests and demonstrations. It placed advertisements in newspapers and national magazines such as *Sports Afield*, *Field & Stream*, and *Outdoor Life*.[7] It even made a promotional film, which it hyped in the February 1965 edition of *Polaris Post*:

Carl Wahlberg (left) and Allan Hetteen test a prototype Mustang at West Yellowstone in 1964. Wahlberg's Comet had been retrofitted with a new cleated track.

This Polaris Voyager is scaling a roof to demonstrate its power. Polaris continued to sell the powerful, rear-engined Voyager into the mid-1960s.

Distributors: Attention! The film "Winter World of Adventure" is the finest piece of advertising you can buy. It features all models of Polaris Sno-Travelers in action in the Challis and Sawtooth National Forest of Idaho, in Yellowstone Park, and even some shots from the Arctic. This film will convince your dealers and prospects that the Polaris Sno-Travelers are all they are advertised to be.[8]

Despite its high profile, the Mustang was just one machine in a growing stable of Polaris snowmobiles. Among the most notable of the Mustang's 1965 stablemates was the L'il Andy, a lightweight snow machine named after its designer, Andy Wells. The L'il Andy was a pared-down sled that fit in the back of a station wagon. David Johnson called it a "great little snowmobile."[9] Also joining the Mustang in the Polaris 1965 line was the Super Pacer, a rear-engined machine that featured the recycled front ends of rejected Comets. "We managed to recover some of the loss on those Comets that way," Johnson recalled.[10]

Still, it was the Mustang that reestablished Polaris's reputation and anchored the company's product line for the next several years. While other models came and went, the Mustang remained. In the 1966 model year, a redesigned version of the Mustang shared top billing with the Colt, a new, lightweight machine designed for speed and maneuverability. The following year, it was joined by a more powerful, "semi-commercial" sled called the Super Voyager.[11] And the Mustang was still going strong in early 1968, when Polaris introduced another lightweight machine, the Charger.

The Mustang years of the mid- to late 1960s marked the beginning of a new emphasis on innovation and quality at Polaris. The Comet crisis had driven home the importance of quality control. Now, with the Mustang, Colt, Super Voyager, and Charger, Polaris was establishing a widespread reputation for superior design and dependability. "The overall appearance has been greatly improved through better design and better tooling," Allan

Hetteen told a meeting of distributors in 1966. "We can now make our machines with much closer tolerances."[12]

But innovation and quality were not the only characteristics that people associated with Polaris during this period. The company also had a well-deserved reputation for speed.

Gaining Speed

It hadn't taken long for racing to become synonymous with snowmobiling and for Polaris to become synonymous with racing. David Johnson had established himself as the first champion snowmobile speedster during his races in the late 1950s against the first-generation Ski-Doos in The Pas, Manitoba. By the early 1960s, snowmobile racing had become increasingly competitive and organized, with large events such as the annual Winter Carnival in St. Paul, Minnesota, sponsoring races and rallies.

In the winter of 1964–1965, snowmobile racing really took off. In late January 1965, about 150 racers—more than triple the number of the previous year—participated in the second annual snowmobile competitions at the St. Paul Winter Carnival.[13] The winners included Roseau native Randy Hites, who drove his blue and white Polaris Mustang to victory in a three-mile competition.[14] The next week, Hites came in first again at the second annual Snowmobile Derby in Eagle River, Wisconsin. One week later, racing was the main attraction at the Roseau Winter Festival. Polaris Mustangs (including one driven by Polaris engineer and emerging racing star Bob Eastman) dominated most of the short-distance races there, although two Ski-Doos outpaced Randy Hites to win what was billed as "the first international snow-machine race in history" between Canada and the United States.[15] Then in late February, Polaris racers, including Allan Hetteen, took away first-place trophies at the Canadian Championship Power Toboggan races in Beausejour, Manitoba.[16]

Speed was quickly becoming an important measure of snowmobile success, and Polaris was up to the challenge. "Polaris is willing to come out in any kind of a contest, speed, endurance, obstacle course races, or what have you, and show the public what their machines can do," Allan Hetteen wrote in the March 1965 edition of *Polaris Post*. But Hetteen was not completely comfortable with the industry's growing obsession with speed. He still believed that the snowmobile's success depended on its acceptance by the general public.

Polaris Mustangs, as well as the other machines, are built to give satisfaction in many more ways than speed. . . . It would seem to us at Polaris that a more sensible feature at the Winter Festivals might be the emphasis on family fun with snowmobiles. Snowmobiles, or "power toboggans" as the Canadians call them, have such a wide variety of uses, some of which are the towing of toboggans and skiers, a conveyance for the hunter, a means to getting into otherwise inaccessible places, and just for the fun of snow traveling. It seems unrealistic to feature the element of speed alone for these snow machines, and we at Polaris would be pleased to see this emphasis changed.

But the industry-wide emphasis on speed did not change. By the winter of 1965–1966, snowmobile races seemed to be popping up wherever the snow fell.

And Polaris—far from abandoning the trend toward speed—embraced it with the introduction of the new, zippy Colt.

The red, white, and blue Colt was shorter, narrower, and lower to the ground than the Mustang, which made it easy to control on the race course. Its smaller two-stroke engines were not as powerful as the Mustang's, but its compact size and improved maneuverability proved to be popular features among the growing ranks of snowmobile racers.

Polaris machines again won first-place trophies at races in St. Paul, Roseau, and Beausejour. They also took top honors in a series of other derbies in places such as Rhinelander, Wisconsin; Livingston, Montana; Barrie, Ontario; Sun Valley, Idaho; Saratoga, Wyoming; Munising, Michigan; and Lancaster, New Hampshire.[17]

Also in 1966, long-distance snowmobile racing finally came into its own. Once again Polaris dominated. In the first running of the 500-mile Winnipeg to St. Paul snowmobile marathon, Polaris Colts finished first, second, and third. The race demonstrated not only the Colt's speed but its endurance as well. Ten of the 15 Polaris machines that started the marathon completed the race. Those numbers compared favorably to the 25 out of 43 ratio recorded by the rest of the field.[18] In Sudbury, Ontario, Bob Eastman took first place in a 160-mile cross-country marathon.[19]

By 1967 snowmobile racing was beginning to show up on the radar of the national news media. *Business Week* called it "the country's hottest new cold weather sport" and reported that more than 100 events were now on the snowmobile racing calendar.[20] Other national publications such as *Sports Illustrated* and the *New York Times* ran articles about racing and the snowmobile industry in general. In almost every case, Polaris—

This page and opposite: Bob Eastman began accumulating racing trophies in the mid-1960s. He continued to race successfully until 1974, when he was nearly killed during a race in Alpena, Michigan.

COAST-TO-COAST COLTS

Clark Dahlin (left) and James Langley begin their transcontinental adventure on the beaches of Vancouver.

IN DECEMBER 1966, TWO UNCOMmonly tenacious snowmobile enthusiasts managed, with Polaris's blessing, to generate more positive publicity for the company than anything Polaris had previously been able to do on its own. Clark Dahlin and James Langley drove two Polaris Colts across the North American continent from Vancouver, British Columbia, to South Portland, Maine—4,018 miles—in 24 days. Newspapers, radio stations, and television stations ate up the story and provided a steady stream of good publicity for the

company. *Sports Illustrated* even ran a feature on the trip.

Dahlin and Langley overcame myriad problems during their journey, few of which were mechanical. Law enforcement personnel in the United States and Canada regularly tried to stop them from driving their Colts on the road, even though the sleds were equipped, like automobiles, with windshield wipers, dual headlights, turn signals, seat belts, license plates, and wheels. Weather was often a problem—too warm at times, too cold at others. And then there were the dogs. "All the way across Canada and the U.S.," *Sports Illustrated* reported, "fine affectionate house dogs, long-known as well-

mannered and beloved pets, came rushing wildly out of yards to try to gnaw on Langley and Dahlin."[1] Dahlin said he gave one particularly hungry-looking German Shepherd "a boot in the face with a Number 12."[2]

Allan Hetteen, for one, was tickled to see how much attention Dahlin and Langley received during their journey. "We're proud of the machines and the record the boys achieved," he said. "We're glad the trip is over so we can go back to building machines instead of checking on where Clark and Jim were most of the time."[3]

Clark Dahlin (left) and Jim Langley cross into Wisconsin after passing the halfway point of their 4,018-mile journey.

Allan Hetteen, seated, poses with his 1966 executive team. From left: Marvin Backlund, Donald Hedlund, David Johnson, Wayne Czek, Bob Eastman, Jerry Reese, Albin Erickson, Dave Bode, Roy Baumgartner, Jerry Thomas, Carl Wahlberg, and Bob Bromley.

with its strong racing credentials—received significant mention.

Polaris's racing success during the mid-1960s and its reputation for innovation and quality created a powerful corporate image that would serve the company well for years to come. Allan Hetteen, David Johnson, and Carl Wahlberg (who was becoming an increasingly integral part of the Polaris brain trust) understood that the ability to stand out from the competition was an important asset. The snowmobile industry was expanding rapidly, and Polaris couldn't afford to get lost in the crowd.

A Popular Pastime

The late 1950s and the early 1960s had been years of struggle and minimal competition in the infant snowmobile industry. "Early sales did not come easy," Carl Wahlberg said. "Polaris and Ski-Doo were in the field alone for the first few years. Most people would look at the machines and wonder which end the snow came out."[21] By 1964, while Polaris was still struggling to recover from the Comet crisis, the industry remained an exclusive club, with Edgar Hetteen's Arctic Cat just beginning to push its way in. Snowmobile sales totaled less than 20,000 a year.

The number of machines sold industry-wide was not all that impressive, but it apparently was enough to create a critical mass. "Once we did get a substantial number of machines out there, it didn't take long to see what a tremendous thing the snowmobile was," Allan Hetteen recalled years later. "Demand took off like a rocket. . . . Overnight there were as many snowmobiles in some of our small towns as there were automobiles. And that's when the competition came into the picture."[22]

By 1965 more than a dozen companies were manufacturing snowmobiles.[23] Overall sales of snowmobiles had climbed to about 30,000 a year. Over the next several years, new companies—Outboard Marine, A.M.F., F.M.C., Thiokol Chemical, Elliot & Hutchins, and many others—continued to jump into the market, and sales continued to multiply. By 1968 the burgeoning industry was selling an estimated 165,000 machines a year,[24] and approximately 280,000 were in current use.[25] The industry spawned a manufacturer trade group (the International Snowmobile Industry Association), an enthusiasts' organization (the International Snowmobile Association), and a specialty magazine (*Snow Goer*).[26]

Expanding Horizons

As the decade progressed and the industry grew, Polaris expanded with it. The company forged strategic partnerships with other firms, opened new facilities, and added to its product line. Some of the moves it made during this period paid off handsomely; others were not so successful.

In 1965 Polaris entered into a short-lived relationship with Larson Industries, a boat maker then based in St. Paul, Minnesota. Larson bought a large chunk of Polaris stock and, for one year, was the company's largest single—although noncontrolling—shareholder. On paper, the arrangement seemed to make sense. Larson's cyclical boat business looked like the perfect complement to Polaris's cyclical snowmobile business. But the partnership never really worked out. "We thought by merging the two companies maybe we could make boats and snowmobiles and grow that way," David Johnson recalled, "but we didn't fit that well together." Although Polaris

did manufacture one season's worth of Larson Hawk snowmobiles, the two companies soon abandoned their merger plans. Polaris bought back Larson's stock in the fall of 1966.[27]

The mid- to late 1960s were also a time of facility expansion at Polaris. In August 1965, the company opened a new assembly plant in Beausejour, Manitoba. The snowmobiles assembled in Beausejour went straight to the Canadian market, allowing Polaris to avoid Canadian tariffs on American-made machines. The new plant also served as a research and development facility.[28] Polaris's expansion continued in 1966 with the addition of a new upholstery plant and paint-drying oven in Roseau.[29] A year later, the company expanded its Roseau operations even further to include a new warehouse and office building.[30]

Polaris also beefed up its product line during this period. In 1966 it began marketing a new "family" of accessories, including snowmobile clothing, helmets, trailers, covers, and tools. "We feel there will be a strong tendency toward more trailer sales and Polaris suits tailored to match the vehicles," Allan Hetteen told a meeting of distributors. The company also began selling its clutch—which it had developed after the Comet crisis—to other manufacturers. "The clutch has been so successful and we've had so many requests to sell it to other manufacturers that we have agreed to market it," Hetteen explained.[31]

The Search for a Better Engine

Meanwhile, Polaris engineers were running a number of tests on engines the company imported from Europe, trying to increase their power. "They were stationary-type, two-stroke engines, and they

Clothing and accessories became an increasingly important part of the Polaris business during the mid- to late 1960s.

didn't develop a whole lot of power," said Jerry Shank, who began at Polaris in 1966 as an engineering consultant and moved into the engine department full time in 1969. "Most of them ran anywhere from 10 to maybe 25 horsepower at the outside."[32]

Having worked at Aero Marine, Shank knew how to coax more power out of boat engines by running them with nitromethane, but he discovered that what worked for a boat didn't necessarily work for a snowmobile.

We had a soup-up shop, where we'd try to get more power out of these two-stroke engines. But we totally destroyed the engines because they weren't designed to run that kind of power. The material wasn't durable enough—the bearings, the rings, the pistons. Most of them were air cooled, and they'd burn up instantly, and that was part of the game: to find ways of making them put power out and still last. It was easier said than done in those days.[33]

Shank used a homemade dynamometer—or "dyno" as the engineers called it—to measure the engine's power. Through trial and error, he and Jerry Endrizzi, the only other man in the engine department, made gradual, though halting, progress. They installed different porting to relieve some of the heat and pressure and installed tune pipes, which, according to Shank, "just about doubled the horsepower." For a few years, Polaris even manufactured a snowmobile with an open hood and fins on the outside to cool the engine with the free flow of air, but that didn't work well either, because it didn't dissipate the heat fast enough.

"We finally concluded that the only way we would be able to put this amount of power through the engine and relieve the heat was to build a liquid-cooled engine," said Shank. "So that's what we did."[34]

Jerry Shank became one of the first engineers to build liquid-cooled engines, which Polaris tested on the racing circuit. The engines were released commercially in the mid-1970s at a time when the company badly needed a product innovation to pull it out of the doldrums. Though the engines were more expensive to produce, the engine department and those on the racing team convinced

the cash-strapped Polaris that speed would sell. "We snuck them out of the dyno rooms and out the back door and did experiments with them," Shank said. "We took one down to Minneapolis and convinced the top managers that speed was the essence of getting people turned on by the snowmobiles."[35]

Meanwhile, while Shank was busy destroying and refining engines, Polaris, in 1966, struck up an enduring and successful relationship with Fuji Heavy Industries, Japan's largest engine builder.

Huch Aoki (back center) and his team at Arrco Industries forged a close relationship with Polaris during the late 1960s. Arrco eventually became a direct subsidiary of Polaris.

Like its competitors, Polaris had always depended on other companies to supply its snowmobile engines. But in the mid-1960s, the company began looking for a single supplier that would work with its engineers to develop an engine made specifically for Polaris machines. In 1967 a Utah-based Polaris distributor named Hachiro "Huch" Aoki approached Fuji on behalf of Polaris.

It didn't take long for the two companies to impress each other. Fuji's executives "had nothing but worldly praise for the people at Roseau and Polaris," Aoki recalled. "It was things like the St. Paul to Winnipeg race, local, regional, and national races, and the fervor of Polaris to remain number one that the Japanese people wanted to be a part of."

The 1967 Mustang came with an optional rear sled for towing passengers, equipment—even Christmas gifts.

Mitchell Johnson, son of David Johnson and nephew of Edgar Hetteen, worked in a number of Polaris positions over the years, including general manager of the ATV division. Mitchell, who in 2002 became responsible for all of the company's engines and transmissions as director of Polaris's Power Train division, described how meticulous Fuji was when it came to giving Polaris what it wanted. "The first engine we sent over to Fuji was one of the German-manufactured engines," he said. "We said, 'We want an engine like this.' It came back, and they had not only copied the engine, they'd even copied the German logo on the bottom of the crankcase."[36]

Fuji started manufacturing Polaris's exclusive "Star" engine in 1968, launching a relationship that would last into the next century.[37]

"Most of our engines before were single-cylinder engines," said Jerry Shank. "Fuji was a bit on the revolutionary side. We went from a single cylinder to a twin, which was a big, big advantage." And though the Fuji engine was air cooled rather than water cooled, Shank said the new engine

"allowed us to have a smaller displacement per cylinder and be able to dissipate the heat better, to develop more power."[38]

Capital Quandary

Still, despite its efforts to expand, Polaris was experiencing increasing difficulties in maintaining market share. By 1968 Bombardier, with its Ski-Doo, was by far the largest snowmobile producer in the world, and Edgar Hetteen's Arctic Cat was challenging Polaris's position as the top domestic manufacturer. Polaris's snowmobile sales, which had totaled just over $1 million in 1964,[39] were now approaching $14 million a year,[40] but that amounted to less than one-tenth of the entire snowmobile market.[41]

Snowmobiling had never been more popular. Sales were nearly doubling every year. But Polaris executives were worried. The company's machines had earned a well-deserved reputation for quality, innovation, and speed. Polaris had expanded through the 1960s as the industry itself expanded. But Polaris was still finding it hard to keep up with the competition.

"We were always struggling and fighting with bankers, trying to get money," David Johnson recalled. "We could see the potential, but how do you capitalize yourself?"[42] As the summer of 1968 approached, Polaris's capital quandary was becoming increasingly acute. Allan Hetteen, David Johnson, and Carl Wahlberg came to a difficult conclusion: they needed to find a buyer—a buyer with deep pockets.

the smooth, speedy, sassy ones for '69!

HOMELITE SNOWMOBILES

Textron's Homelite division sold three different Polaris-made snowmobile models: the Ranger, the Forester, and the Explorer.

CHAPTER FIVE

BIG BUSINESS

1968–1971

Industry pundits agree the boom is near its peak. And they conclude that of today's 40 manufacturers, only the toughest, smartest and best financed . . . will survive.

—*Forbes* magazine, February 1970

I N LATE MAY 1968, THE POLARIS board of directors met in Roseau to decide the company's fate. Two large conglomerates, Textron Incorporated and LTV Corporation, had made offers to buy Polaris. Executives at both firms could see that the snowmobile business was exploding and wanted to get in on the action. By this time, most of the Polaris board members had come to agree with Allan Hetteen—that selling the company made sense. Now they just had to decide which offer to accept.

On paper the decision looked easy. LTV had outbid Textron. But money was not the only consideration. All of the board members were either from Roseau or had strong ties to the community. They worried that Polaris's new owner might move the company to another town and wanted to prevent that from happening if at all possible.

The board members weighed the pros and cons of both offers. LTV would pay more, but Textron, they believed, was more likely to keep Polaris in Roseau. The discussion went back and forth, and eventually the majority settled on LTV.

But that was not the final word. Allan Hetteen, David Johnson, and Carl Wahlberg remained the three most powerful voices on the Polaris board, and the other board members agreed to defer to them. "The three went out of the room to decide, and the board said they would sell out to whomever

the three decided on," recalled board member Jim Helgeson. "They decided on Textron."[1]

"Employees and the community were always extremely important to my dad," said Allan's son, Mike Hetteen. "The Textron offer was the lower dollar amount, but Textron had the most commitment to the community and to the people who depended on Polaris to make their living."[2]

The decision had been made, but the papers had yet to be signed. Mike Hetteen remembered the rather unusual closing of the deal.

Polaris was nearing the end of negotiations, getting ready to sign the papers with Textron, but things weren't finalized yet, and we had a family vacation planned up at Lake of the Woods that my dad had been looking forward to for a long time. He wasn't willing to give up his family vacation and said that if Textron needed to have the papers signed when he was on vacation, then they would have to come out to the islands and find him.

The 1969–70 lineup, including the all-new TX series, helped Polaris stage an impressive comeback after a disappointing performance the previous year.

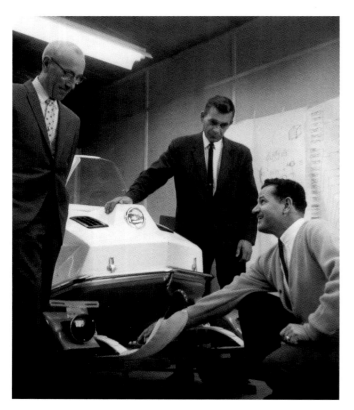

Carl Wahlberg (left) looks over a 1969 Mustang with Roy Baumgartner (center) and Bob Bromley.

Well, Textron decided they wanted the papers signed. We were up in the Sioux Narrows area, and Carl Wahlberg, along with people from Textron, flew out in a floatplane and landed on the island. They sat down in a tent, reviewed the documents, and that's where they were signed.[3]

On July 31, 1968, Polaris stockholders approved the company's sale to Rhode Island–based Textron, whose subsidiaries already included Bell Helicopter, Shaeffer Pens, Hallmark Cards, and Homelite. Under the purchase agreement, Polaris shareholders received 0.71 shares of Textron common stock in exchange for each Polaris share. With approximately 300,000 Polaris shares outstanding and Textron trading at over $50 a share, the deal was worth around $11 million. In announcing the sale, Allan Hetteen expressed confidence that Textron would keep Polaris in Roseau and make the investments needed to push the company forward.

I feel it is a solid step toward strengthening Polaris and making our base more solid. It will give us diversification as we will have access to vast financing if we see a good product we can manufacture. . . . We are much more apt to have year-around employment here and I believe it will strengthen the local economy tremendously because of not only the year-around employment, but the outside money which is available, and the ready access to technology, know-how and research in any number of lines Polaris independently would have difficulty in obtaining.[4]

With most decisions about the upcoming 1968–1969 snowmobile season already made, Textron seemed content to do as little tinkering as possible at Polaris. "We have complete confidence in the present Polaris management team to further build their position in the snowmobile industry," said Textron president G. William Miller.[5]

Allan Hetteen, David Johnson, Carl Wahlberg, and the rest of the old guard at Polaris would get a chance to show Textron what they could do. Unfortunately for them, the upcoming season would not live up to expectations.

1968–1969: An Off Season

By the end of the summer of 1968, Polaris seemed poised for great success. Textron was now at the helm and promising to make significant investments in its new snowmobile subsidiary. Polaris had just opened a new production facility in Afton, Wyoming, and a new, $3 million expansion of the Roseau plant, including a 14-station oval assembly line, was now complete. The expansion was necessary, Allan Hetteen explained, "to meet the market demands for Polaris products."[6] About 500 employees were working at the newly updated plant, and the company anticipated hiring another 200 before the year was out. Polaris had also opened a new warehouse in Minneapolis to expedite deliveries and had recently doubled its fleet of trucks and trailers.[7] The company was capitalized and expanding. It was ready to battle for a considerably bigger share of the snowmobile market.

Gaining that extra market share, however, was not going to be easy. More than 20 companies, including Yamaha, Ariens, and Massey-Ferguson, were jumping into the snowmobile fray with 1969 models.[8] The growing competition of the mid-1960s was not letting up. Still, Polaris was determined to rise above the competition on the retail level and on the racetrack.

It was unsuccessful on both counts.

On the retail side, Polaris made the mistake of getting option-happy. Its 1969 snowmobile line gave customers more choices than they had ever had before. It included just four basic models: the Mustang, Colt, Voyager, and the all-new Charger. But the machines came with a choice of 22 different engines from six different manufacturers—Wankel, Hirth, Sachs, JLO, Kohler, and Fuji (which was just ramping up its production of the exclusive Polaris "Star" engines). The variety of engine options may have appealed to consumers, but dealers were not amused. Faced with the prospect of stocking parts for 22 different engines, many Polaris dealers abandoned the company and switched to competitors—especially Arctic Cat.[9]

The vast number of options put a dent in quality control as well. Tool room supervisor Clayton Carlson was a staff engineer at the time and remembered how difficult it was to get all the product releases necessary before manufacturing could begin. "I sat down and made out a chart that included all the different chassis types, suspensions, tracks, engines—all the different types. When we took all those elements into consideration, we discovered we were producing 244 different models. The quality suffered because we couldn't focus our attention on all those different models."[10]

The 1968–1969 season was just as hard on the Polaris racing program. In November the company showed off its new TX racing models at a grass drag racing derby in Beausejour, Manitoba. (Racing on grass was a novelty event that was just beginning to catch on.) Despite high expectations, the TX machines performed only moderately well. Over the next several months, Polaris racers, who had gotten used to dominating the field, increasingly found themselves in the "also-ran" category. The engines on the TXs were not as good as the team had expected. The machines themselves were too heavy. The old bogie wheel

Dennis Olson clears six automobiles in a leap with a Polaris snowmobile during a performance of the Polaris Thrill Show in Detroit Lakes, Michigan, in February 1969.

suspension that had carried Polaris to racing dominance was obsolete.[11]

Polaris tried to make up for its retailing and racing setbacks by putting more money and effort into promotional campaigns. Among its most successful efforts was the Polaris Thrill Team. Team members, led by public relations director Ted Otto, drove specially modified machines that crashed through burning walls, spun around 360-degree loop-the-loops, and jumped over long lines of cars. In February 1969, the thrill team helped generate extra publicity for the company when it appeared at Nevada's Ponderosa Ranch, home of the popular television western *Bonanza*. The Polaris machines were especially popular with Dan Blocker, the actor who played Hoss Cartwright. After several hesitant circles on a Polaris 634, Blocker "opened it wide open and roared across the snow," Otto said. "He thought it was really wild."[12]

Still, the Thrill Team's public relations successes couldn't hide the fact that the 1968–1969 season was a major disappointment for Polaris. The

Top: The Polaris Thrill Team, headed by Ted Otto, generated positive publicity for the company during its short but colorful life. The team disbanded amid safety and liability concerns. From left: Dennis Olson, Ted Otto, Allen Kukowski, Loren Miller, and Roger Dick. (Larry Rugland not pictured.)

Above: The 1970 Playmate came with an optional wheel kit that allowed owners to use their machines during the summer as well as the winter.

company needed better consumer machines and better racing machines if it expected to prosper in the increasingly competitive snowmobile market. It was time to go back to the drawing board.

1969–1970: Mixed Bag

In June 1969, Polaris unveiled its new snowmobile line for the 1970 model year. The lineup was, Allan Hetteen insisted, greatly improved and simplified.

This year we are cutting down on some of the options and are offering a lot of accessories as standard equipment on our machines. We are stressing quality, serviceability, strength and the most machine for the customer dollar. . . . We are determined that in our machines, the customer will be getting the best machines in the world.[13]

The 1970 product line included a new lightweight sled called the Playmate. It also featured a line of "high performance" machines designed to appeal to racers and racing fans. The TX series, as it was called, capitalized on several design innovations developed through the Polaris racing program, including the company's exclusive Torque-O-Matic clutch system. The TX line featured three models: the TX Playmate, the TX Charger, and the TX Colt. Each one came with a choice of engines from a variety of manufacturers. Despite Allan Hetteen's claim to the contrary, the Polaris product line was still option-heavy, especially when it came to engines.

The company set what Allan Hetteen called a "pretty ambitious" goal for the 1969–1970 season: a 50 percent increase in production and sales. Other snowmobile manufacturers were setting their sights lower, anticipating a leveling off in the market. But Polaris executives seemed confident that the 1970 models would come through.

Textron backed up Polaris's ambitious goals with a $2 million expansion and modernization program at the Roseau plant. The program included, among other things, a new research and development building for the company's engineers, draftsmen, racing team members, and quality control personnel. By November 1969, labor on the expansion was nearly complete, and about 1,000 employees

BONANZA

DURING THE WINTER OF 1968–1969, Polaris scored a publicity coup when it successfully linked its name to one of the most popular television shows of the time: *Bonanza.*

Huch Aoki, Polaris's Utah-based distributor, established the link by working out an agreement with the Ponderosa Ranch—a popular tourist attraction near Lake Tahoe and the television home of *Bonanza*'s fictional Cartwright family. Under the agreement, Aoki supplied the Ponderosa Ranch with several dozen Polaris snowmobiles to help the ranch attract winter tourists. In return, Polaris received loads of favorable publicity, including photographs of *Bonanza* stars Lorne Greene, Dan Blocker, and Michael Landon posing with Polaris sleds. Aoki called Polaris's *Bonanza* connection "one of the single most significant things that put Polaris on the map."[1]

Polaris Thrill Team riders Ted Otto (second from left) and Dennis Olson (second from right) pose for a publicity shot with *Bonanza* stars Dan Blocker (center left) and Michael Landon (center right).

The Star Car gave snowmobile owners a way to use their snowmobile engines year round.

were at work on the 1970 models. "We think the new facility will enable us to do a better job, be more efficient and have better controls on production quality," said Hetteen.[14]

At the same time, the Polaris race team was gearing up for what it hoped would be a much more successful racing season. Bob Eastman, who had been named race team manager the previous spring, had led the development of a new, aluminum TX racer featuring the company's first true slide-rail suspension.[15] The new machines had performed extremely well in the autumn grass races, and hopes were high that their early successes

would translate into more trophies and increased sales on the retail level.

Behind the scenes, Textron was beginning to shake up the small-town culture that had defined Polaris since its inception. In November 1969, Textron brought in Herb Graves, former president of its Gibson Electric subsidiary, to serve as executive vice president and general manager of Polaris. In February 1970, Polaris announced it was moving its administrative office to an existing building in Minneapolis and that Graves would be based there. These moves raised concerns among Polaris's well-established Roseau contingent, but Allan Hetteen insisted there was no cause for worry. "[The Minneapolis] office puts our company in the mainstream of the snowmobile industry," he said. "It is a must if we are to continue to strengthen Polaris's position within the snowmobile industry and to seek out and develop other product lines for Polaris to manufacture."[16]

The development of a new product to complement the snowmobile was becoming an obsession of sorts at Polaris—and at Textron. "We have a goal of at least one or two products for the market next spring [1970]," Hetteen said. The company was trying to determine whether there was a market for its experimental Star Car—a diminutive racecar that ran on a removable snowmobile engine. It also was testing a large, dual-tracked snow-and-swamp utility vehicle that it called the Model 6000.[17] Both machines showed promise, but Textron was reluctant to commit to either of them.

As the 1969–1970 season progressed, Polaris saw reason for optimism and pessimism. Bob Eastman's new TX racers, with their slide-rail suspension systems, were burning up the race circuit, but the company was falling well short of its 50 percent sales increase goal. In fact, sales were merely holding steady at an estimated 25,000 units a year.[18]

Nerves were increasingly on edge. Throughout the snowmobile industry, the word on everyone's tongue seemed to be "shakeout."

"Industry pundits agree the boom is near its peak," *Forbes* magazine reported. "And they conclude that of today's 40 manufacturers, only the toughest, smartest and best financed . . . will survive."[19] Allan Hetteen agreed. "I feel there will be a shakeout," he said, "and some [companies] will fall by the way." But, Hetteen added, Polaris would not be among them.[20]

In with the New

As it turned out, Allan Hetteen would not get the opportunity to lead Polaris through what most observers believed was an imminent shake-out in the snowmobile industry. On June 1, 1970, Allan Hetteen stepped down as president of Polaris Industries. "The doctor says I should take it easy for a while," he told the local newspaper. "This opens up a new era in my life when I can do some of the things I have dreamed about and not been able to do. I hope some of the ideas I've had can become realities now.... Perhaps there will be a little more time to devote to them." He planned to continue working as a consultant and a Polaris distributor.[21]

Hetteen's retirement marked a significant changing of the guard at Polaris and a further shift away from the company's Roseau roots. Textron initiated the transformation by naming Herb Graves president and announcing that Graves

Above: The Star Car, being examined here by (from left) Allan Hetteen, Huch Aoki, and Carl Wahlberg, elicited high hopes initially, but the project survived only a few years.

Below: Newly retired Allan Hetteen (left) visits the Polaris research and development shop with Textron president Bill Miller (center) and Polaris's new president, Herb Graves (right).

SAFETY AND NOISE

BY THE LATE 1960S, THE SNOWMO-bile's growing popularity was helping to create a slew of public relations headaches for Polaris and the rest of the snowmobile industry. The nonsnowmobiling majority was getting tired of plugging its ears to the "great racket" created by the machines' noisy two-stroke engines.[1] And many people, both in and out of the snowmobile industry, were becoming increasingly alarmed about the growing number of snowmobile accidents. In October 1968, Polaris announced a pair of initiatives that helped establish the company as a leader in snowmobile safety and noise control.

The centerpiece of the new Polaris safety program was a package of educational materials made available to snowmobile clubs, public service organizations, and media outlets. Allan Hetteen said he decided that Polaris needed to take the lead in safety education after serving as president of the International Snowmobile Industry Association. "I came to the conclusion," he said, "that we manufacturers had to do more

to educate the public in the responsible use of our snowmobiles."

Polaris's noise reduction efforts were, at first, couched in safety terms. In fact, Carl Wahlberg downplayed the growing public outcry over noise as he announced that the company's 1968–1969 models would feature a new and "dramatic silencing system."

"We are convinced, he said, "that a quieter machine will enable the driver to hear what is going on around him, like car horns and voices, thus avoiding many possible accidents."[2]

Over the next several years, Polaris continued to make its snowmobiles safer and quieter. By 1973 the news media were reporting that innovations such as sealed-beam headlights and nonsticking throttles were significantly improving snowmobile safety.[3] In 1974 Polaris created a new Sound Engineering Department to respond to new sound reduction laws in Canada and several states. Those laws mandated that snowmobile manufacturers reduce the sound levels of their machines to 82 dB in 1975 and 78 dB in 1976.[4]

Safety issues became very important at Polaris during the late 1960s and early 1970s.

Polaris Reflective Tape
"spotlights" hazards along your trail!

■ To nighttime snowmobilers, wire and other small objects are almost invisible. Now, by using Polaris Safety Tape and by traveling at a reasonable speed, these trail hazards can be readily seen by normal snowmobile headlights in plenty of time to stop or turn.

Carry a roll of Polaris Safety Tape in your snowmobile and mark the dangerous wire and other obstructions along the trails frequently used.

But remember, the best insurance against accidents at night is reasonable speed and caution, especially when running in an unfamiliar area.

It's easy to use Polaris Safety Tape

would run the company from Polaris's new corporate headquarters in Minneapolis. (Longtime managers Carl Wahlberg and David Johnson would stay in their current positions in Roseau.) Other outsiders added to the management team included former Philco-Ford marketing executive Francis McGrath as marketing director, former Minneapolis-Moline plant manager Thomas Fuchs as director of manufacturing, and the former president and CEO of Master Builder, George Schaffer, as director of operations.[22]

Graves's promotion and the opening of the Minneapolis headquarters sparked new rumors about the future of Polaris's Roseau operation. In November 1970, Graves sought to extinguish those rumors in an address to the Roseau Civic and Commerce Association.

Our financial investment and our investment in people is far too great to move. We frankly could not sell the [Roseau] facility for nearly the investment we have in it . . . and we could not transfer the expertise of the people without losing the heart of the business.[23]

Textron would be "deluding" itself, Graves said, if it thought it could successfully run Polaris without the help of the many people in Roseau who had built it up over the years.

1970–1971: Comeback

As the 1970–1971 snowmobile season approached, the new Polaris management team expressed confidence that the company would come back strong after two years of stagnant sales. "We feel we will easily increase at a faster rate than the rest of the industry," predicted new marketing director Francis McGrath. "We will pick up the market from those who do not make the long-term commitment to the future we have made."[24]

Polaris was placing its bets on a new line of consumer sleds that drew more than ever before on

design enhancements developed by the company's racing program. The 1971 TX-series machines all featured the "Power-Slide" suspension system that Bob Eastman's race team had pioneered during the previous season. And all of Polaris's 1971 snowmobiles—the Charger, the Mustang, the Voyager, the Playmate, and the TX sleds—came with Polaris's exclusive Star engines. No longer did Polaris dealers have to stock parts for myriad engines built by five or six different companies.

By the end of 1970, it was becoming increasingly clear that Polaris was heading for a monster year in 1971. Its sleds continued to rack up wins on the racing circuit, and its 1971 consumer models were selling like never before. After two years stuck at about 25,000 units sold, in 1971 Polaris was on a pace to sell more machines than in any other year: an estimated 30,000.[25]

Polaris's new management team and its 1,000 or so employees had engineered an impressive comeback during a year when a lesser company could easily have degenerated in the throes of a corporate shakeup. The Textron-ization of Polaris appeared, at least for the time being, to be a major improvement over the old days, when capital was always in short supply. "We spent more time before . . . finding money . . . than running the business," Carl Wahlberg observed. "Now we can tend to business."[26]

The 1970–1971 season was a high point for both Polaris and the snowmobile industry. Total industry sales for the year approached 500,000 units.[27] But no one in the snowmobile business was resting easy as the season came to a close. The heady years of 50 to 100 percent sales growth were over. Inventories of unsold machines were at an all-time high. The International Snowmobile Industry Association now counted nearly 100 manufacturers in the snowmobile business.[28] More than ever before, the industry appeared to be setting itself up for a fall, and Polaris and its new management team were bracing themselves for the coming concussion.

President Herb Graves (left), plant manager Ron Payne (center), and production vice president Tom Fuchs were all smiles as the last 1972 Polaris rolled off the assembly line. Little did they know that the entire snowmobile industry was setting itself up for a fall.

CHAPTER SIX

JOSTLING FOR POSITION

1971–1981

Sometimes when it looks bleak it turns out a lot better than one might expect.

—Arnold Ochs, vice president of manufacturing, 1981

TO THE CASUAL OBSERVER, Polaris looked to be in an excellent position in 1971. Its machines were restyled for the 1971–1972 season, and production was near an all-time high, with nearly 1,000 employees working at the Roseau plant. Things were going so well that the company was having a hard time finding qualified employees. "We need every person we can get in here," Carl Wahlberg said.[1]

In October 1971, Polaris formalized the corporate restructuring that had begun the year before. Francis McGrath, Thomas Fuchs, and George Schaffer were all promoted to vice president. Ron Payne was named production plant manager. And in a significant shift from the company's past, Carl Wahlberg eased away from his previous responsibilities and became special assistant to the president. (He officially retired in March 1973.)

"Our growth has made necessary more specialists in more areas and a reduction of responsibilities," Herb Graves said, summing up the new appointments. "We need to train and upgrade our present people and to get specialized skills from outside for expertise in certain areas."[2]

In November the company completed the move into its new corporate headquarters in Minneapolis. Polaris, it seemed, was ready for what Graves called the "next generation of growth." That growth, however, would be accompanied by substantial growing pains.

Off and Running

Polaris's high hopes for the future turned out to be well founded—if only for the short term. Sales for 1971 were up 60 percent from the previous year, without, according to the *Roseau Times-Region,* dealers having to resort "to extensive price-cutting or year-end dumping."[3]

Unfortunately, the industry as a whole was beginning to stagger. For the first time, snowmobile sales industry-wide actually declined—from nearly 500,000 in 1970–1971 to approximately 460,000 in 1971–1972[4]—and carryover inventory remained uncomfortably high at around 150,000 units.[5]

Dark clouds were gathering on Polaris's horizon as well. In March 1972, Sears, Roebuck & Company, which had sold Polaris snowmobiles under the Sears label during the 1971–1972 season, unexpectedly announced that it was getting out of snowmobile sales.[6] In June Polaris narrowly avoided its first labor strike when union

The 1977 TX-L was a breakthrough machine for Polaris. Its unique liquid-cooled engine was superior to its competitors', and its aluminum extrusions acted as foot warmers.

Above: Engine specialists from Fuji Heavy Industries made frequent trips to Roseau as Fuji and Polaris built a close relationship throughout the 1970s.

Below: On March 14, 1970, Polaris gained the upper hand in racing when Mike Baker (pictured) pushed the experimental X-2 "Flying Wedge" to a world record of 109.9 miles per hour during a run in West Yellowstone, Montana.

members approved a new three-year contract one day after the previous contract expired.[7] (The company had inherited the union when Textron purchased Polaris.)

Still, Polaris exuded confidence as it strode into the 1972–1973 model year. The Mustang, Colt, and Charger were reengineered and restyled to reflect the streamlined design of the company's racers, and the TX 335 was introduced to keep would-be speed demons happy. When asked why Polaris was making so many changes after a record-breaking sales year, Herb Graves responded, "Because we want to follow one record year with another one and because you don't maintain leadership by sitting back and enjoying last year's success."[8]

In October the company launched a $500,000 expansion aimed at making its machines safer. "The emphasis here as in the rest of the additions will be safety," said plant manager Ron Payne. "We are making a prime effort in the area of safety as well as in the area of ecological protection."[9]

When the 1972–1973 production run ended in December, Polaris announced that its manufacturing volume was now double what it had been in 1969; it was manufacturing about 55,000 machines a year.[10] In addition, Polaris announced that its inventory of unsold machines was down. "We are in good shape this year," Ron Payne said. "Our factory inventories are below last year . . . with more machines in the hands of dealers."[11]

Fixing a Hole

But by the end of the 1972–1973 season, sluggish sales clearly indicated that the snowmobile industry as a whole had grossly overproduced. Sales were down to about 450,000 machines, leaving approximately 300,000 left unsold.[12] Polaris—whose share of the carryover inventory had actually decreased during the 1972–1973 model year—was now at the mercy of a glutted market.

In early 1973, Textron responded to the changing market conditions in the snowmobile industry by shaking up Polaris's organizational structure. The parent company merged Polaris into a single division with its E-Z-Go golf cart subsidiary, promoted Herb Graves to another Textron division, and replaced him with Beverly Dolan, E-Z-Go's president and founder. In a letter explaining the

IN MEMORY: ALLAN HETTEEN

ALLAN HETTEEN HAD KEPT HIMSELF very busy since retiring in 1970. He had gone into business independently as a Polaris distributor, had helped establish a local surplus company, and had built a large farming operation that he called the "Diamond H Ranch." He had taken a seat on the board of a Roseau bank and had kept active in several civic and professional organizations. He had remained one of Roseau's most respected citizens. But on November 24, 1973, Allan Hetteen's life was cut short.

He died while helping a neighbor.

Hetteen was driving a large front-end loader back to his farm after backfilling over a neighbor's septic tank. The road was icy, and the big machine began to swerve. It slipped into a ditch and flipped on its back, crushing its driver. Allan Hetteen was 44.

The local newspaper, the *Roseau Times-Region,* ran the story on its front page. "The accident," it reported, "ended the still-growing career of one of Roseau County's most popular and able young men."[1]

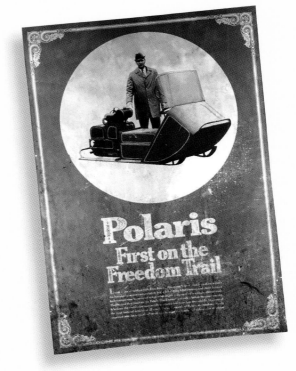

Polaris cofounder Allan Hetteen died on November 24, 1973, three years after his retirement.

restructuring, Graves assured Allan Hetteen that Textron remained committed to Polaris and the snowmobile business. "Polaris will continue to give major emphasis to the snowmobile market," he wrote. "Snowmobiles will account for the majority of Polaris sales for years to come."[13]

The upheaval at Polaris occurred just as the national news media were picking up on what they called the snowmobile "crunch." As *Business Week* reported, "The industry has three basic problems. Overproduction is pinching profit margins. . . . Snow has been spotty in prime market areas for three winters. And public outcry over safety and environmental hazards has restricted the use of snowmobiles in some states, including Massachusetts and New York."[14] Henry Fiola, editor and publisher of *SNOWsports* magazine, predicted, "There will be realistic production cutbacks for 1974 models. It will take a couple of years to get production back into phase with the market."[15]

As it turned out, the situation was much worse than Fiola had forecast.

A Melting Industry

In October 1973, war broke out in the Middle East, and the Organization of Petroleum Exporting Countries (OPEC) slapped an embargo on crude oil shipped to the United States. Fuel shortages quickly developed, and long lines at U.S. gas stations became commonplace. On November 7, President Richard Nixon appeared on television and asked all Americans to conserve energy by lowering their thermostats, driving their cars more slowly, and eliminating unnecessary lighting. As winter approached, it became increasingly clear that the nation was facing a severe energy crisis.

Left: Dorothy Mercer and Roma Walker run neck and neck at the 1973 "America's All Year Playground" snowmobile races in South Lake Tahoe, California.

Below: The early 1970s were the years of the snowmobile industry's "speed wars." Here Mike Baker rides the X-2 "Flying Wedge."

The timing couldn't have been worse for the snowmobile industry. November and December were traditionally the two biggest months for snowmobile sales. Manufacturers were hoping that a strong showing during the early part of the 1973–1974 season would help them slash excess inventories. But the nation's growing energy fears kept potential customers away from showrooms. Sales plummeted. Even the racing circuit suffered as officials canceled half of the season's scheduled events.[16]

Polaris was sucked into the vortex with the rest of the industry. "The timing of the energy shortage situation was incredibly bad from our standpoint," Bev Dolan said. "Bam! . . . Sales stopped for about 30 days and then picked up again when we got some snow and the government said there'd be no rationing, but a month of prime selling time was gone."[17]

In January 1974, Polaris began hunkering down for what looked to be a potentially devastating downturn. "When the energy crisis broke in early November, our dealers experienced a slowdown in retail snowmobile sales," Tom Fuchs reported. "This, combined with the excess industry inventories and late snows for the third straight year, have caused us to be very cautious in planning our new 1975 model production schedules." Polaris announced a 25 percent cut in its managerial staff and hinted that full-scale production for the coming year could be delayed indefinitely.

In a news release, the company tried to calm fears that Polaris might go under. "With the backing of Textron," it said, "Polaris has the ability to ride out any temporary market slow-down created by the energy shortage. . . . We will just have to wait it out and see what the second half of the year brings as far as an increase in overall snowmobile sales in the industry."[18]

Three months later, the full extent of Polaris's retrenching efforts became clear. Production on the company's new line of 1974–1975 models (including the Colt, Colt SS, Electra, TC, and TX) began under a severely reduced manufacturing schedule. The Roseau factory ran just one shift, and the company insisted that that single shift would easily cover the anticipated demand. "Our production for the [1974–1975] season has already been sold," Ron Payne reported. Polaris was offering its distributors limited supplies of machines, a strategy designed to encourage inventory reduction and help the company "start next year with a clean slate."[19]

"During that period of the oil embargo, nothing worked, no matter what we did," remembered Chuck Baxter, who began his Polaris career in 1970 as a project engineer and later became vice president of engineering. "We were in an environment where many, many companies were trying to stay alive, whether through a price promotion or a new product, but there were always companies doing more and then going out of business."[20]

With the Roseau plant running at well below capacity, the company began looking for manufacturing opportunities outside the snowmobile realm. In the summer of 1974, it started producing space heaters for Textron's Homelite division. The following winter, it launched production of the E-Z-Go GT-7 golf course maintenance vehicle. The two products allowed Polaris to keep the Roseau facility open—albeit on a single shift—nearly year round.[21]

As Polaris struggled to keep its head above water, many of its competitors in the snowmobile industry were sinking. Sales for the 1974–1975 season were down again, to approximately 316,000,[22] and leftover machines from the previous year accounted for many of those sales.[23] More and more manufacturers—including Outboard Marine's Johnson and Evinrude divisions and Suzuki—announced they were getting out of the business.[24]

This thinning of the snowmobile ranks presented new opportunities for Polaris, even as it struggled to survive. Bev Dolan predicted that only about eight manufacturers, including Polaris, would survive the industry shakeout. "We are bound to pick up a percentage just by being there," he told a meeting of the Roseau Civic and Commerce Association. "It all adds up to good business for Polaris."[25]

Polaris kept its goals modest as the 1975–1976 season progressed. The Roseau plant continued to run on one shift, but the company announced plans to increase its peak payroll to about 500 employees, an addition of about 80 more than the previous season.[26] Once again, production of the Homelite space heater and the E-Z-Go maintenance vehicle helped fill holes in the Roseau production schedule.

While the 1975–1976 season turned out to be yet another difficult one for the snowmobile industry (sales dropped again, to 243,000),[27] Polaris emerged in relatively solid financial shape. Bev Dolan called the season "one of the banner years in the history of the company." The secret, according to Ron Payne, was the company's conservative approach to the market. "We're producing approximately half of our ultimate high in units," Payne said, "but we're making more money, about twice . . . what we made in 1974, the year the whole industry

Casual yet classy—the 1975 Polaris safari suit had the look of exciting adventure.

took a dive. . . . It's a more logical, more organized business [approach], completely adjusting to what the market really is."[28]

A Brave New World

The 1976–1977 season marked the start of a three-year period of recovery and consolidation in the snowmobile industry. By the summer of 1976, the hard times of the previous several years had knocked out all but six manufacturers: Polaris, Bombardier, Arctic, John Deere, Scorpion, and Yamaha. All six were scrambling to pick up market

The 1976–77 Polaris Professional Cross-Country Race Team: (from left) Bob Przekwas, Ed Monsrud, and Burt Bassett. This was the first season Polaris fielded its own professional cross-country team.

share from the companies that had fallen by the wayside, and all six were hoping that the market itself would soon start growing again. Carryover inventory had dropped to 82,000,[29] and industry leaders expressed confidence that the managers of the surviving companies would never again fall into the trap of overproduction. "If they're businessmen, then they have to have learned from the past," said Mortimer Doyle, president of the International Snowmobile Industry Association. "I really doubt that they'll get into that kind of bind again."[30]

At Polaris, executives were looking forward to better times. "There is every indication that 1976 should be a good year," Bev Dolan declared in May. "Production started up smoothly and is progressing well."[31]

A month later, the company's growing optimism was interrupted by another shakeup at the top. Textron promoted Dolan to head up its Homelite division and replaced him with David F. "Fritz" Myers—Polaris's fourth president in six years.

While Polaris maintained its modest one-shift production schedule, it also continued to innovate. In the summer of 1976, it introduced what turned out to be one of the most groundbreaking machines in its history. The TX-L was a consumer sled that incorporated several innovative technologies developed by the company's racing team. Topping the list of TX-L innovations was its twin-cylinder liquid-cooled engine. Other companies had experimented with liquid cooling before this, but the TX-L's cooling system was different. Instead of a standard radiator, it relied on aluminum extrusions mounted under the running boards. This unique design also produced a welcome side benefit: the system's circulating water kept riders' feet warm.[32]

"We started dominating the racing circuit," said Jerry Shank, who was one of the original designers of the twin-cylinder, liquid-cooled engine. "We were blowing everyone away, and it was like taking candy from a baby. But it wasn't just the engines that made us better. The chassis got better, the clutches—it was a combination of everything."[33]

Polaris limited the production of the TX-L and its other machines (including the new Cobra) that season, which turned out to be a smart move. Industry wide, sales during the winter of 1976–1977 dropped to 195,000, their lowest level in nine years.[34]

Polaris called the 1980 TX-L Indy a "hot iron that takes the wrinkles out of the trail." It was the first consumer sled to feature Polaris's race-tested independent front suspension.

Still, sentiment was growing that the industry had finally bottomed out and had nowhere else to go but up. A new manufacturer, Kawasaki, was jumping into the business, and the other survivors were positioning themselves to take advantage of what they hoped was an improving business climate.

At Polaris, production for the 1977–1978 season actually dropped slightly as the company nurtured its growing zeal for inventory control. Management was preparing to make a grab for market share from a position of strength. In a speech to the Roseau Civic and Commerce Association, president Fritz Myers assured his audience that Polaris would be around "for a long, long time. . . . Polaris is still here and increasing its share of the market."[35] Myers's optimism was well founded. When the season wrapped up in March 1978, the numbers showed that Polaris and the rest of the industry had increased sales for the first time since 1970.[36]

The 1978–1979 season showed even more improvement. The snowmobile industry reacted to its success of the previous year by significantly boosting production, and sales continued to rebound.

Polaris approached the 1978–1979 season more conservatively than its competitors did. While production at the Roseau plant increased by two-thirds, Myers insisted that the company was maintaining what he called "controlled growth"— a plan aimed at increasing market share while controlling year-end inventory. And the plan worked. The 1978–1979 model year was, in the words of one magazine, "a near sellout."[37]

Shrinking inventories, snowier winters, and an improving economy had helped Polaris and the remaining snowmobile manufacturers (Arctic had by this time acquired Scorpion) to rebound nicely from the frightening years of the mid-1970s. The companies began preparing for even better times, but they were in for a rude surprise.

Independent Front Suspension

Polaris was pinning much of its hope for the 1979–1980 season on a new machine featuring a

A DEATH IN THE RACING FAMILY

POLARIS HAD BEGUN fielding its own factory racing team in the late 1960s, and its riders—Bob Eastman, Jim Bernat, Larry Rugland, Stan Hayes, Leroy Lindblad, Dorothy Mercer, and others—had done more than anyone else to establish Polaris's reputation for performance and speed. But in 1978, Polaris abruptly dropped its factory racing program after suffering a death in its racing family.

Jerry Bunke was one of three Polaris drivers known collectively as Midnight Blue Express. Wearing midnight blue uniforms, Bunke and fellow team members Steve Thorson and Brad Hullings dominated the racing circuit on RX-Ls with stylized red, white, and blue hoods. (The RX-L was the prototype of the TX-L independent front suspension sled.)

Snowmobile historian Jerry Bassett called Bunke a consistently smooth rider—"the supreme embodiment of a golden age of snowmobile racing."[1] On February 26, 1978, Bunke was killed during a race at the Canadian Power Toboggan Championships in Beausejour, Manitoba. Three months later, Polaris announced that it would no longer sponsor a factory racing team, although it would continue to support independent racers.

The company had been contemplating a change in its racing program for some time, but Bob Eastman believed Bunke's death was the final straw. "They already knew that they wanted to go from a three-man successful team down to one-man development," Eastman recalled, "but when Jerry died, I think they got afraid. They felt liability exposure and so forth."[2] Publicly, the company downplayed the liability aspect, stressing instead the benefits of independent racing. "We believe," said vice president of engineering John Dwyer, "that extending our factory racing support efforts to all Polaris independents, rather than focusing solely on two or three factory drivers, is a good change for Polaris and is in the very best interests of the industry."[3]

Jerry Bunke, "the supreme embodiment of a golden age of snowmobile racing," died in a tragic racing accident on February 26, 1978.

technological breakthrough developed, once again, on the race circuit. Bob Eastman remembered working on the prototype.

We worked hard to make sure the entire package worked well, not just the IFS [independent front suspension], but the engines, the clutches, the rear suspension to go along with it, the whole chassis. The whole idea is to absorb the bumps and keep the skis on the snow or ice, to get the front end flat and be able to control it better. The prototype was called the RX-L, and we tested it in Alaska in 1976. It wasn't perfect yet, but we could sure see the potential.[38]

Three years later, Polaris released the TX-L Indy, a consumer sled with a new, race-tested IFS. Snowmobile manufacturers had been trying for years to come up with an IFS that actually worked at full throttle. Polaris was confident that it had finally succeeded.

"We believe the Indy is the premiere trail sled in the industry," said John Dwyer, vice president of engineering. "It may also win races, but it has been designed and manufactured to deliver the most comfortable, stable, and fastest ride on moguled terrain."[39] As Dwyer suspected, the Indy did win races; in fact, it dominated the 1979–1980 race circuit. But it didn't live up to expectations in the showroom.

Murphy's Law

Then again, neither did any other machine. The winter of 1979–1980 was a disaster for the snowmobile industry. Nearly everything that could go wrong for snowmobile makers did go wrong that season. Snowfall was way down, inflation was way up, and the nation was mired in another energy crisis. Inventories of unsold machines were once again piling up. Polaris tried, despite dealers' objections, to protect itself by paring back its production goals as winter approached, but it still manufactured more machines than it had the year before. And many of those machines went unsold.

By February 1980, the snowmobile industry was facing a new crisis. Polaris began laying off salaried employees and announced plans to slash production 50 percent during the upcoming 1980–1981 season. "The production period of work will be shorter than it has been the last couple of seasons," reported Arnold Ochs, vice president of manufacturing.[40]

Pam Hetteen (her husband is first cousin to Edgar and Allan Hetteen) worked in the human resources department when Polaris started downsizing. Of her nearly 30 years at Polaris, she remembered that time period as the toughest. "People would walk by my office and look in, and it was almost like they were looking to see if they would be next," she said. "I knew who was going to be next, and it was really hard."[41]

Through it all, Polaris's strong, family-like atmosphere remained intact. Ken Wojciehowski, who started at Polaris in 1968 as a welder and later became service parts coordinator, remembered how management, and Arnie Ochs in particular, cared about employees and their families.

It was about 1980, and my daughter had cancer, so I'd take off early on Friday afternoon. Arnie Ochs was always checking with me to make sure everything was okay. He came up to me one day before I was leaving, and I felt him pushing something in my pocket. He said, "Don't tell people about this" and walked away. I'm wondering what the heck he did. I get into my car and found that he'd put $500 in my pocket.[42]

Years after his retirement, one of Ochs's most lasting memories of Polaris was the people: "I'd been at several different companies prior to coming to Polaris, and without question, the people who I met and worked with at Polaris were the most talented and capable and dedicated people I've been associated with. It gave me a great sense of pride and enthusiasm to work in that environment."[43]

In Search of a New Course

A few days after announcing the cutbacks, Polaris made another announcement: It had a new president. Fritz Myers had left to take a job with another firm. Taking his place was 37-year-old W. Hall Wendel Jr., previously vice president of sales and marketing and a man who loved the great outdoors. A graduate of the Naval Academy and Harvard Business School, Wendel had spent

Hall Wendel joined Polaris E-Z-Go as a salesman in 1972 and quickly rose through the ranks. Textron named him president of the division in 1980.

four years in the U.S. Navy and joined Polaris in 1972 doing sales in the E-Z-Go division.

In an interview with the Roseau newspaper, Wendel tried to downplay speculation that Polaris was in danger of folding. "This was an unusual year with little snow in the snowbelt," he said, "but yes, I am optimistic. We need to get away from the poor weather and the slow economy. Next year will be a little better and after that it will get good again." Textron, he said, remained "committed to the snowmobile industry."[44]

In fact, Textron was desperate to get out of the snowmobile business, though as David Johnson pointed out, "Textron could have closed us up immediately, just walked out of there, but they ultimately helped Polaris stay in Roseau."[45]

In an interview less than two years after being named president and CEO of the company, Hall Wendel described what was really going on behind Textron's closed doors:

Textron was just evaluating where it was and where it wanted to go, and Polaris didn't fit. Because of the weather, and the economy, the snowmobile industry can be an up-and-down situation, and Textron is interested in steady increases from year to year. Textron originally bought Polaris when the snowmobile industry was a growth industry. It's no longer a growth industry.[46]

Wendel's first job was to oversee a drastically reduced production schedule for the 1980–1981 models. The new line included a new, lower-cost machine called the Cutlass (the only new snowmobile model introduced by any manufacturer that year), but its introduction was overshadowed by the company's 50 percent production cut. The production run, which in most years lasted into

December, was, at first, scheduled to end in mid-October. But as the recession deepened during the summer, the company announced plans to lop off an additional four weeks. Arnie Ochs said the company had determined that consumers were now in a "buy only the necessities and beat debt" mode.

We recognize the added financial loss to Polaris and the hardship to the employees and community, . . . but we had a strategy of restricting the losses to one year and avoiding an inventory carryover in 1981. We don't feel that our initial cutback was sufficient to accomplish that. The 1980 model inventory is what we want to sell out so we reduced the 1981 build.[47]

Wendel's second big job during this period was to find a buyer for Polaris. In the months following his elevation to the company's top spot, he brought several potential suitors to Roseau, but in the end only one of them made an offer: Polaris's oldest rival—Bombardier, the maker of Ski-Doo.

Polaris and Bombardier went public with their courtship in September 1980, hoping to put to rest a variety of rumors that were running rampant in Roseau at the time (including one involving a possible sale to Greyhound Bus Lines).[48] In a prepared statement, Hall Wendel tried to reassure the people of Roseau that the proposed sale would have "a positive impact on the area's economy in the future."[49] Bombardier president Lou Hollander said he wanted to buy Polaris from Textron (he was not interested in E-Z-Go), and let Polaris operate as an autonomous division based in Roseau.[50] The two companies hoped to finalize the deal in October.

A few weeks later, however, the deal was dead. Arctic called the proposed buy to the attention of the U.S. Justice Department, which dropped strong hints that it would reject the sale on anti-trust grounds. Polaris and Bombardier agreed that, given the government's opposition, the acquisition would be more trouble than it was worth. In the words of Hall Wendel, "Both Textron and Bombardier chose not to contest the opposition because of the uncertainty and excessive expense that would result."

In typical Polaris spirit, many of the remaining employees at the Roseau plant expressed their

The Polaris Cutlass was the only new snowmobile model introduced by any company during the 1980–81 season.

relief. "Once we found out that [the sale] wasn't going to happen, someone got the idea that we'd create some tee shirts," recalled Mary Zins, who started working for Polaris in 1979 and later became manager of human resources. "They were red in color, and they said on it, 'I'm glad we didn't DOO it.' We all wore our tee shirts very proudly."[51]

In Search of a Silver Lining

The situation at Polaris was now "business as usual," said Arnie Ochs.[52] But "business as usual" was nothing to celebrate as far as Polaris and its competitors were concerned. Snow was sparse once again during the winter of 1980–1981,

and snowmobile sales were anemic. In January 1981, Polaris announced that it planned to cut production by an additional 40 percent for the 1981–1982 season. Ochs tried to soften the blow by comparing the company's current situation to the hard times it had experienced in the early to mid-1970s. "It was pretty bleak," he recalled, "but it came back from there. Sometimes when it looks bleak it turns out a lot better than one might expect."[53]

The 1983 Indy Trail headlined Polaris's new line of Indy sleds and gave trail riders a chance to enjoy the benefits of independent front suspension. *(Photo courtesy* Snow Goer Magazine.*)*

CHAPTER SEVEN

CARVING OUT A FUTURE

1981–1983

We are not going to limit ourselves. We are going to look at different areas—agriculture, consumer products, industrial products. We want to take full advantage of the engineering, manufacturing, sales, and marketing resources of the company.

—Hall Wendel, Polaris president and CEO, 1981

THE SPRING OF 1981 BROUGHT A vague sense of dread to Polaris employees in Roseau and Minneapolis. Textron had made it clear with the Bombardier sale attempt that it wanted to get out of the snowmobile business. Polaris was now officially up for sale, and no one could predict with any certainty how, or even whether, the company would survive.

In late March, the Roseau newspaper reported that "bankers representing a potential buyer" had come to check the company's books and assess its facilities.

For its part, Polaris tried to put the best spin possible on its uncertain future. "It is encouraging from the standpoint that there is interest out there in the purchase of Polaris," Arnie Ochs said.[1] Still, employees were on edge. On several occasions they found themselves "cleaning up the plant for another executive tour." Rumors began spreading about who the possible suitors might be. Some guessed Kawasaki. Others guessed John Deere.[2]

But as March turned into April, Polaris still had no buyer.

On April 6, 1981, about 140 employees at the Roseau plant started work on a limited run of the 1981–1982 models. Fewer than 6,000 machines were produced, most of which were essentially the previous year's models with new decaling. In

just six weeks, the work was done. All but about 13 people at the Roseau plant were laid off.

"That was a very scary time," said master scheduler Lloyd Fugleberg, one of the 13 employees lucky enough to keep working. "Most of the people who stayed knew a little bit about a lot of things. Maybe they could drive a forklift, load a truck, run the computer."[3]

"We pulled some double duty," said David Dokken, who started in Polaris's paint department in 1963 and later became senior purchasing agent. "I recall doing a night shift in the guard shack. We'd also tear our different products apart and try costing them to see what we could do if we got back into the business."[4]

The few who remained provided corporate life support as well. "We mowed our own lawns," said longtime employee Bud Olson. "I was even changing the toilet paper in the bathrooms. Everybody was doing whatever they could."[5] The company's attitude, recalled Chuck Baxter, was to wait for autumn and "hope that it snows."[6]

Polaris's early ATV team did everything it could to get Cenex interested in private-label ATVs, but Cenex wouldn't bite. *(Photo courtesy Gary Olson.)*

"Polaris is still awaiting developments regarding its potential purchase," the company's May newsletter reported. "A group of Roseau citizens has been making efforts to locate prospective buyers and has been working with both Polaris and Textron to this end."[7] This was the public line, but more was unfolding behind the scenes. Few people inside or outside the company realized that a group of familiar names from within the company was already preparing to come to the rescue.

Independence Day

Hall Wendel, the new president and CEO, who had been told by Textron to find a buyer for Polaris, was running out of options. Textron was still committed to finding a buyer that would continue manufacturing operations in Roseau, and none of the companies that had expressed interest in Polaris were willing to promise to keep the company viable in the snowmobile industry.[8] As each potential deal disintegrated, Wendel began considering another option. What if he and a group of Polaris managers scraped up enough capital to buy the company? Would Textron bite? Wendel—now thinking of himself as a buyer, not a seller—took a hard look at the deal Textron and Bombardier had worked out the previous fall. The harder he looked, the more excited he got. "We realized, hey, this is an attractive package," Wendel recalled. "It is a good buy for people who can manage it."[9]

Wendel began assembling a group of Polaris and Textron executives who were willing to take the substantial risk that a purchase of Polaris would require. The group included Chuck Baxter, vice president of engineering; Arnie Ochs, vice president of manufacturing; John Fiebelkorn, vice president of sales; Keith Libbey, secretary; Bruce Rushton, Polaris E-Z-Go's vice president of marketing; Robert "Bob" Moe, the vice president and general manager of Textron Financial Corporation; and David Johnson, the one man who had been with Polaris since its beginning. Wendel also brought in an outsider with considerable experience in corporate takeovers: his father, William H. Wendel Sr., former president and vice chairman of the $2 billion Kennecott Corporation.

Hall Wendel and Bob Moe met with Textron president (and former Polaris president) Bev Dolan to discuss a possible deal. "It was late afternoon, so we went to a bar," Wendel recalled more than 30 years later. "We outlined the deal on the back of a table napkin in about 10 or 15 minutes. We signed it, and Bev signed it, and he gave it to the lawyers the next day."[10]

The management team's leveraged buyout (LBO) deal, according to Wendel, "was pretty much the same deal that had been offered to any other companies that were interested, but nobody was interested, apparently."[11]

One of the main challenges of any LBO is debt service—how to pay down the debt and accrued interest involved in buying the company while still maintaining positive cash flow. "Our initial goals were pretty simple, and they were aimed at surviving," Wendel said.

So we focused on three things: first was cash flow, not necessarily profitability, to cover the debt. Number two, we took a lean-and-mean attitude toward running the business, trying to conserve expense and overhead wherever and

Below left: Chuck Baxter, vice president of engineering, was one of several Polaris managers who pooled their resources to buy Polaris from Textron in 1981. He began working at Polaris in 1970 as a project engineer.

Below right: Arnie Ochs was also among the managers who bought Polaris from Textron. Ochs joined Polaris in 1975 and served as the company's vice president of manufacturing during its last two years under Textron.

Above left: Hall Wendel, who became Polaris's president and CEO at the age of 37, led the company through some of its toughest years. "We are ready, we are organized, we have the people in place, we know what we want to do," Wendel said at the announcement of the buyout from Textron.

Above right: Bob Moe was another manager who joined in buying Polaris from Textron. Moe joined Polaris as controller in 1970 and was named vice president and general manager of Textron Financial Corporation in 1978.

whenever possible. Third, we focused on our strength, which is product innovation, and that's always been the hallmark of Polaris.[12]

The strategy worked. Within three years, Polaris would pay off all its debt to Textron, and within six years, Polaris would go from number four in the snowmobile business to number one. "And we've been number one ever since," Wendel said.[13]

Despite Polaris's eventual success, when Wendel, Moe, Baxter, and the others first bought the company and racked up a debt-to-equity ratio of 20:1, none of them were certain that the company would survive.

Lloyd Fugleberg summed up events from the employees' point of view: "One day we got fired by Textron and came in the next morning and got hired by Polaris."[14]

The atmosphere was festive outside Polaris's suburban Minneapolis headquarters on July 21, 1981. Food and refreshments were served under an open tent while a band played music in the background. Smiles stretched across nearly every face as Hall Wendel announced the deal he had worked out on a napkin only a few days earlier:

We are convinced there will always be a snowmobile business. It might not be as robust as it once was, but it will be there, and we want to be part of it. Our group, which has been involved with the management of Polaris, knows the company's strengths and we know the snowmobile business. We thought this was a good opportunity. . . . We have trimmed some expenses and eliminated the fat, but the muscle remains. We are ready, we are organized, we have the people in place, we know what we want to do.[15]

At the time the sale was announced, Polaris was down to 46 employees—34 in Minneapolis and 12 in Roseau. But to those who remained, the day of the announcement was a day to remember. "We were saved on July 21st of 1981," Mary Zins recalled more than 20 years later. "It was kind of a pivotal date that nobody will ever forget."[16]

"For a while there Polaris didn't look very promising," said Udell Nelson, product coordinator for the snowmobile division, who started with Polaris in 1962. "But our top management did a super job; they're really what brought this company around."[17]

By all accounts, Hall Wendel was a tough but fair boss, a hands-on leader who was concerned with every aspect of the business. No challenge was ever too great for the daring outdoorsman, who had climbed to the top of the tallest mountain on every continent, including two trips up Mount Everest. Come what may, Wendel was determined to see that Polaris succeeded.

Strategy for Success

In the weeks following the sale, the new ownership team worked feverishly to devise a business plan that would ensure the company's short-term and long-term survival.

"Our modus operandi, being we had no money, was that we weren't going to make anything we couldn't sell," said Bob Moe. "We pretty much sold everything all the way through, not just to dealers, but through the dealer to the customer."[18]

Aside from being conservative, a key component of Polaris's survival plan was diversification—the development of products besides snowmobiles. Hall Wendel had declared at the July 21 news conference that Polaris would soon "be marketing and manufacturing an ever broader range of products."[19]

"We are not going to limit ourselves," Wendel said. "We are going to look at different areas—agriculture, consumer products, industrial products. We want to take full advantage of the engineering, manufacturing, sales, and marketing resources of the company."[20] Nearly everyone agreed that the company would "die on the vine" if it had to continue praying for snow.[21]

Bob Granitz, design supervisor of the snowmobile division, remembered driving 80 miles to Crookston with Chuck Baxter, Bob Eastman, and others to a winter festival showing the latest in farm machinery. "We spent the whole day there looking for little things that we could build," he said. "We were trying to dream up things that Polaris could manufacture—anything to make money."[22]

Bruce Rushton, Polaris E-Z-Go's vice president of marketing and a member of the management buyout group, drives an E-Z-Go golf cart. The newly independent Polaris would continue manufacturing clutches for Textron's E-Z-Go golf cart division into 1989.

"We needed another product to keep the plant open year round and get the overhead down, and there were many things that were looked at," said Lloyd Fugleberg. "We looked at an ultralight airplane factory in North Dakota, looked at air-seeder farm equipment—looked at anything. But at the time, the farm economy was down, and there wasn't anything that looked promising."[23]

Polaris's first foray into diversification was really nothing new. In October 1981, the Roseau plant began manufacturing clutches for Textron's E-Z-Go golf carts. The plant had been making clutches for E-Z-Go for several years, but the autumn production run marked the beginning of a new relationship between the newly independent Polaris and its former owner. "This is the first in what Polaris hopes will be a continuing and growing number of such contracts which can provide production for the Polaris facility and employment opportunities for the Roseau community," Ochs said.[24]

Meanwhile, Polaris was seeking to diversify in two much more substantial ways: development of new products and acquisition of other products and companies.

All-Terrain Proves Tough

Polaris engineers didn't have a whole lot to do in Roseau during the summer of 1981. The plant's 1981–1982 production run had ended in May, and unresolved ownership questions made it impossible to make firm decisions about the next year's snowmobile models. So the engineers started doing what good engineers do when they have time on their hands; they started tinkering. The object of their tinkering was a three-wheeled all-terrain vehicle (ATV) similar to the machines that several Japanese companies had recently introduced in the United States. "We had recognized the ATV was a product line that is kind of similar [to the snowmobile] in terms of people going out of doors and playing," Chuck Baxter recalled, "so we started experimenting."

Baxter, along with engineers Norm Berg and Jan Hedlund, spent most of their summer "monkeying" with the new machine behind closed doors on a "skunk works" basis. "We talked about whether we should be investing in it or not," said Baxter.

"The general consensus was that we shouldn't be, but we did keep it alive, even though we weren't supposed to."[25]

By the time autumn rolled around, the group of engineers believed that they might really be on to something—that the ATV might be the new product Polaris was looking for.

But Hall Wendel wasn't so sure. "Hall didn't have the confidence to make bigger investments," Baxter recalled. So Baxter made a suggestion: What if he could convince another company to contract with Polaris to produce "private label" ATVs? Wendel liked that idea. "If you can convince someone else out there to do it," he said, "we'll go along with it."[26]

Baxter and his team produced two prototype ATVs—a green and yellow one designed to hook John Deere and a red one made to attract the giant farm cooperative Cenex. In October 1981, Baxter and Bruce Rushton traveled to Portland, Oregon, to try to convince Cenex to place an order for 1,500 units, but Cenex wasn't interested. "So we just killed the private label idea," Baxter recalled.[27]

Still, Baxter wouldn't give up. "He kept trying to sell the ATV idea to others within Polaris," recalled Bob Nygaard, then manager of sales and marketing administration, "and he kept getting told, 'No, this doesn't make any sense. We're not going to go there.'"[28]

By early 1982, Baxter's ATV was officially on hold. "Basically the project rested for a couple of years without a lot of activity," Baxter said. "We weren't even actively working on it."[29]

Polaris's diversification efforts were now focusing on acquisitions.

Chasing the Cat

Arctic Cat—Polaris's longtime rival started by Edgar Hetteen in the nearby town of Thief River Falls, Minnesota—had emerged from the 1980–1981 snowmobile season in even worse shape than Polaris. Unlike Polaris, Arctic had tried to build itself out of the industry-wide sales slump and had ended the season with a huge inventory of unsold machines. In the spring of 1981, while Polaris was still looking for a buyer, Arctic Cat filed for bankruptcy. In November its creditors and shareholders approved a reorganization plan under which Arctic would sell off its snowmobile operations.

Bob Nygaard, later to become general manager of snowmobiles, assisted in rebuilding the Polaris dealership network during the first few years of the company's independence from Textron.

Arctic was on the selling block, and Polaris—still struggling to gain its footing under new ownership—couldn't disguise its interest. "I guess it's no secret that we've been kicking the tires up there a little bit," Bruce Rushton admitted.[30]

Here was an opportunity that seemed almost too good to pass up. If Polaris played its cards right, it could acquire a valuable brand name while simultaneously removing a rival. Polaris managers started crunching the numbers.

On December 16, 1981, Polaris and Arctic announced that they had signed a letter of intent under which Polaris would purchase Arctic's entire snowmobile operation. "The Arctic Cat snowmobile, Arcticwear clothing, parts and accessories line will be continued essentially unchanged as a separate product line," Hall Wendel announced. "This is an important step for Polaris Industries," added William Wendel Sr. "It allows us to acquire what we want—more market share, key personnel specialized in the Arctic product line, a strong dealer organization, loyal consumers and an excellent name, without buying what we do not need—the fixed assets." Both companies emphasized that the deal was not final. Details still had to be worked out.

As it turned out, the devil was in the details. Less than two months later, on February 5, 1982, Polaris and Arctic announced that the deal was off. In a press release, the two companies claimed that they had been unable to complete the transaction in time for Polaris to make its "manufacturing and purchasing commitments" for the coming year. "Time simply ran out on us," Hall Wendel said.[31]

Wendel's public statements masked disagreements within Polaris. Some members of the company's management team wanted to go ahead with the deal, if only to make sure that Arctic could never come back. But they were overridden. "We backed off at the last minute," recalled Chuck Baxter, "largely because Hall was a little afraid, and I think he thought that [Arctic was] dead anyway, that they wouldn't make it back."[32] (As it turned out, Arctic Cat did reemerge as a successful brand after a group of former Arctic executives purchased the manufacturing rights in 1982.)

In the months to come, Polaris would continue to publicly express its commitment to diversification through acquisition. "We are continuing to study diversification as an alternative since the collapse of the proposed purchase of Arctic," said Arnie Ochs in April 1982. "There is nothing positive to announce yet, but we are confident we can achieve diversification and provide job stabilization at Polaris for the future."[33]

In June Hall Wendel announced that the company was pursuing "three or four prospects."[34] Six months later, he claimed, "We have a lot of things on the burner . . . but nothing on the front burner yet."[35] Finding companies and products to acquire was turning out to be more difficult than Polaris executives had anticipated.

Taking Care of Business

Even as Polaris looked to diversify through acquisition and product development, it never forgot that the snowmobile remained its livelihood. Hall Wendel in particular believed that the com-

EMPLOYEE RELATIONS

TWO SIGNIFICANT AND LASTING changes in Polaris's relationship with its employees began in 1982. One involved union representation. The other involved employee compensation.

In July of that year, Polaris employees voted to decertify the International Woodworkers of America union, which had represented them since the 1960s.

"We feel that this is the most effective way to improve company-employee relations," a company spokesman said. "Current economic conditions clearly indicate that American manufacturers must be efficient and produce quality products if they are going to survive in today's marketplace."[1]

Two months later, Polaris announced that it was instituting a profit-sharing plan. "It is a way for each of us to prosper as the company prospers," Arnie Ochs said.[2] In that first year of profit sharing, Polaris distributed $200,000 to approximately 500 employees. The amount of profit sharing increased so dramatically during the following decade that by 1992, the company was distributing more than $6 million each year (and that didn't include the value of the employee ownership rights that the company began distributing after going public in 1987). "The profit sharing was the best," Mary Zins recalled. "It really tied us together as a team. It motivated us to pull together for the company's success."[3]

The combination of union decertification, profit sharing, and stock ownership was a boon to most employees. "[W]hat they've got now is all the benefits [of the union] and the stock and the profit sharing," said David Johnson. "Why, they're way ahead and they don't pay union dues."[4]

The Indy 600 was one of two liquid-cooled, independent front suspension machines in the Polaris 1983 Indy line. *(Photo courtesy Snow Goer Magazine.)*

pany had to find new ways to build on its reputation for snowmobile quality and innovation while keeping costs under control.

"Hall was a very hands-on manager," Bob Nygaard recalled. "He fully understood that new product was the lifeblood of snowmobiles. He was also very sensitive to cost. Hall's leadership was to continue to invest in product, watch every nickel that we spent, and run a very lean organization."[36]

And Polaris did, indeed, watch every nickel. As an example, the carpeting in the Minneapolis headquarters building had not been replaced for decades and was striped with tributaries of duct tape to make it wear longer. Bob Moe, in charge of the company's finances, once overheard a new employee asking why Polaris didn't replace the carpeting. "This carpet is reversible," Moe quipped. "We're going to turn it over and get another 50 years out of it."[37]

Wendel himself summarized his philosophy in concise and straightforward terms: "We are gearing up to make money so we can operate tomorrow."[38]

In June 1982, 375 Roseau employees began production on new 1982–1983 models. Polaris was, by this time, one of only four remaining snowmobile companies (the other three were Bombardier, John Deere, and Yamaha), and it was a much leaner company than it had been during its years under Textron. "It's obvious," said Ochs, "that

we're a new company, not only in our management philosophy, but [in] the products we offer and how we promote them."[39]

Although Polaris managers were not yet aware of its significance, 1982–1983 was the first model year in which the company offered a broader line of "Indy" independent front suspension snowmobiles. During the previous two seasons, Polaris had built a limited number of Indys, all of which were liquid-cooled machines designed for high-performance riders. Now the company was more than doubling its production of Indys and was expanding the Indy line to include the fan-cooled Indy Trail, a machine that "gave trail riders all the benefits of Polaris Independent Front Suspension without the added cost of liquid-cooling."[40] In addition to the Indy Trail, the company offered two liquid-cooled sleds, the Indy 600 and the Indy Cross Country.

"Indy" was turning into a recognizable brand. This was, according to Chuck Baxter, a significant development for a company that had previously failed to come up with an effective branding strategy.

Ed Skomoroh, who started with Polaris in 1982 and soon became vice president of sales and marketing, introduced Arctic Cat–style "sizzle" to Polaris's marketing efforts.

We'd think that our marketing was effective, and we'd have a theme of the year. Next year, we'd have a different theme. The consistency in branding wasn't there previously. We'd have models called TX and TX-L and Colt and Cobra—all different kinds of names that had to do with—What did they have to do with? Was it letters? Animals? When we came out with independent front suspensions, they got nicknamed Indys, and when we came out with a model, it became known as an Indy. The name really focused our promotion. It wasn't just the engineering we were touting; it was also the presentation. We were selling Indys.[41]

The ascendance of the Indy brand occurred at about the same time the company was beginning to pay more attention to other aspects of marketing. Early in 1982, Hall Wendel had hired former Arctic Cat executive Ed Skomoroh to head up Polaris's Canadian operations. Wendel was clearly hoping to tap into the wider sales and marketing expertise that Skomoroh had developed at Arctic—a company with a reputation for marketing "sizzle."

Skomoroh was glad to offer his opinions. "I told Hall I thought we had a great product,"

Skomoroh remembered. "We had a great motor, great suspension. But the vehicle was ugly and overpriced, and we didn't have a dealer network. Hall said, 'Well, fix it.' "[42]

Pricing had long been a problem for Polaris. The price tags on its machines had consistently been on the high side—no matter the niche. Now, with prodding from Skomoroh and the company's sales and marketing group, Hall Wendel was shifting Polaris's pricing policy. From then on, the company would concentrate on selling "premium value machines at extremely competitive prices."

"I really give credit to Hall Wendel for his insight on pricing," Baxter said. "Textron would provide a product and typically price it in the upper third of the price distribution. Hall moved that down to the lower part of the distribution, so we're underpricing the competition."[43]

At the same time, the company was revamping its dealer network. By December 1982, it had cut loose about 35 percent of its dealers and, in many cases, replaced them with Arctic Cat dealers.[44] Bob Nygaard considered this change to the dealership infrastructure an important factor in Polaris's future success.

We had a list of North American Arctic Cat dealers, and we would go through them one at a time and compare them to the Polaris dealers. We knew what they sold in terms of whole goods, parts, garments, and accessories, and we knew, rudimentarily at least, their financial strength. We'd compare them to Polaris dealers, and we'd make some strong recommendations to our independent distributors that they look at upgrading their dealer base utilizing these Arctic Cat dealers. The Arctic Cat dealer network was, as a general comment, perhaps a little more professional than Polaris's. They were better marketers, more capitalized.[45]

From Three Steps to Two

Around the same time, Polaris was transitioning from a distributor-based network to dealer-direct distribution. "We became closer to our customers—i.e., the dealers—by having a direct relationship with them instead of going through distributors," said Nygaard. "By that time, we were the only snowmobile manufacturer that was still dealing with independent distributors, and it put us at a disadvantage. Changing our dealer base after Arctic Cat went out of business was one of the major reasons for Polaris's success. That and the independent front suspension were the two things that really drove our snowmobile business through some lean times."[46]

Though good business necessitated the switch, Skomoroh was quick to point out that distributors such as Larson-Olsen, in Minneapolis, R. L. Ryerson, in Wisconsin, Nelson and Small, in the Northeast, and Western Power Sports, in the West had been vital to Polaris's survival as it struggled in the early 1980s. "We truly needed distributors because we didn't have the cash flow, and when you sell a snowmobile to a distributor, you get paid immediately."[47]

Skomoroh first tested the dealer-direct distribution system in Canada, then launched it in the United States. "We immediately started picking up more dealers," said Skomoroh, who was quickly promoted to vice president of sales and marketing. "The dealers knew that by cutting out the middle man, they'd be getting more programs regarding systems and advertising and that we'd be able to massage the retail prices and increase the discounts for the dealer."[48]

Skomoroh explained the importance of dealers when it came to selling a product. "You need the dealers' support," he said. "You can have a great product, but if you don't have channels of distribution, nobody's going to buy them. The dealers we ended up going with were good businessmen, and they knew the Polaris name, knew the brand, and believed in the reputation of the product."[48]

Wanda Campbell, sales administration manager, explained how drastically the company changed once it began revamping its dealer network.

We basically went from 12 customers to 1,000 because each of those 12 distributors had dealers we took on. Then we hired sales managers, which we had never had before, who went out and solicited hundreds more dealers. And all of a sudden we started hiring people to do marketing and advertising to a direct dealer base. That's vital because our dealers are probably the most important link in our business.[49]

Nygaard further strengthened this revamped dealership network by instituting a new system under which dealers were regularly surveyed to find out how many machines they had in inventory and were retailing. By the spring of 1983, data generated by those surveys indicated that Polaris's share of the snowmobile market was steadily increasing (by 5 percent in the United States and by 8 percent internationally) and that inventories were well under control. "I feel very good about our current position," Nygaard said.[50]

Still, Polaris had plenty of reasons to worry. Industry-wide sales during the 1982–1983 season had dropped to a historic low of approximately 87,000 sleds. In essence, the company's growing market share represented a slightly larger slice of a shrinking pie. And not only that—the company's continuing efforts to diversify through acquisitions and product development had still failed to bear fruit.

Fortunately, that was about to change.

External relations manager Marlys Knutson oversaw development of Polaris's "Believe It" marketing campaign during the early 1990s.

CHAPTER EIGHT

LEARNING NEW TRICKS

1983–1993

*If we were going to keep growing, we had to do something dramatically
different. We had to start expanding.*

—Ken Larson, president and COO

AS PRODUCTION OF THE 1983–
1984 models got under way
in June 1983, Polaris executives continued to chant the diversification mantra. "We know how
important it is to our employees to
have longer employment and to the
success of the company [that we not]
rely on a single product," Arnie Ochs
told the Roseau newspaper. "At the same time we
don't want to make a mistake that could endanger
the production we do have." The company was still
casting about for new products that would allow it
to take full advantage of its production capabilities
and provide year-round employment for its workers. But, as Ochs put it, "We haven't been able to
complete a transaction."[1]

Mike Malone, who began working for Polaris
in 1984 and later succeeded Bob Moe as CFO,
remembered his hesitancy about hiring on at a
snowmobile company. "1984 was only a few years
after all the snowmobile companies had gone out
of business," he said. "There was a fear of being
the last passenger on the *Titanic*."[2]

Malone soon realized that Hall Wendel and
Bob Moe had already brought Polaris out of danger, but the company was still a "hand-to-mouth,
season-to-season operation for several years," he
said. "We didn't even bother to finish our budget
until after the snowmobile orders came in the spring.
The snowmobiles drove the whole business."[3]

Finally, in early 1984, Polaris's
diversification efforts began to pay off.

In February, the company
announced that it had agreed to take
over the snowmobile operations of
one of its three remaining competitors, John Deere, which wanted to
divest itself of snowmobiles and
concentrate on farm implements and
lawn and garden machines. Under the agreement,
Polaris would manufacture John Deere snowmobiles at the Roseau plant and would continue to
supply parts, service, and clothing to John Deere
snowmobile dealers. "This is an important first
step in bringing additional products to Roseau,
while strengthening our position in the snowmobile industry," Hall Wendel said.[4]

Polaris never did manufacture John Deere
snowmobiles (dealer orders fell well below the
number needed to justify production), but it did
acquire parts, inventory, and—most significantly—
a new roster of dealers with "a reputation for good
service."[5] Polaris cherry-picked the best Deere dealers and added them to a dealership network that
kept improving, thanks in large part to the addition
of some former Arctic Cat dealers.

Hall Wendel led Polaris through its diversification efforts and
into a new era of growth.

At about the same time that Polaris was acquiring John Deere's snowmobile operations, it was moving into a whole new business: paint sprayers. In early 1984, Polaris purchased Graco's Roto Flo line of consumer-grade paint sprayers and announced plans to manufacture the little machines in Roseau. Hall Wendel said production of the sprayers would help the company achieve year-round employment at the Roseau plant.[6] As it turned out, demand for the Roto Flos was anemic, and the company dumped the product after only two years of production.

Even as Polaris touted the John Deere and Roto Flo acquisitions, behind the scenes it was reviving plans for another product with much greater diversification potential. The all-terrain vehicle (ATV) was not only back on the Polaris drawing board; it was barging into the company's collective consciousness.

Reinventing the Wheelers

Hall Wendel had shelved Polaris's all-terrain vehicle program in early 1982 after the failed attempt to forge a partnership with Cenex, but ATV supporters within the company, including Chuck Baxter, had never given up on the concept. In the summer of 1983—with encouragement from his father, Polaris CEO William Wendel—Hall Wendel agreed to revive the ATV program with a modest $100,000 investment.[7]

Over the next several months, Baxter, Bob Eastman, and the rest of the ATV design team developed three different all-terrain machines: a three-wheeler with a Yamaha drive line and a Polaris body (Yamaha agreed to supply the drive line, Baxter said, because it "had a guilt feeling about driving all these U.S. companies out of business"); a three-wheeler with a Polaris drive line and a Polaris body; and an all-Polaris four-wheeler.

In the spring of 1984, Baxter snuck the new machines into a distributors meeting to gauge interest. "We started by bringing one or two of the distributors over to the side and kind of showing them the ATVs in this other room," he recalled. "Before the show was over, we were showing them on the floor and asking our distributors what they thought, whether or not they were interested."[8]

EDGAR HETTEEN RETURNS

AFTER NEARLY A QUARTER CENTURY away from the company he founded, Edgar Hetteen returned to Polaris in January 1984, this time as official company spokesman. Hetteen had spent much of the previous 24 years with Arctic but decided to move back to Polaris after a group of investors resurrected the Arctic Cat brand under the new Arctco Industries umbrella. Hall Wendel hailed the appointment, saying that "no living individual has played a larger part in establishing and building the industry as Edgar Hetteen and we are proud to have him again as a part of the Polaris team."[1]

The distributors were definitely interested, but only in the all-Polaris designs. Baxter and his team went back to work. They dropped the Yamaha drive line and concentrated on homegrown technologies. With their background in snowmobile design, they naturally incorporated familiar features such as two-stroke engines and the Polaris Variable Transmission (PVT), an automatic transmission. The PVT gave the Polaris ATV an advantage over competitors because it was simpler to handle. The engineers also added unique features, including floorboards (instead of motorcycle-like foot pegs) and MacPherson strut suspensions.

Dean Hedlund, ATV development supervisor in charge of troubleshooting new products, explained how the floorboard innovation came about.

There's a real benefit to just going out and having fun with the machine like a consumer would do. We developed a full floorboard concept because a couple of guys were out, and they happened to slip off the conventional foot pegs that everybody else was using and hurt their ankles. So we said, "You know, this isn't right." So we put a big floorboard on it, and since then, the industry has followed our lead.[9]

Finding ATV dealers in the snowbelt region was not a problem because many of them already sold Polaris snowmobiles or at least knew of Polaris's reputation for quality. But finding ATV dealers in the South was more difficult, according to Ed Skomoroh.

No one had heard of us. They'd heard of Polaris Pool Sweeps, but of course we weren't a pool company. So we took on dealers who were selling used cars and used farm equipment, and some of them, lo and behold—because they didn't have negative, preconceived ideas about our product features versus the competition's—really got behind us. But when we tried to join up with Honda and Yamaha ATV dealers in the South, it didn't work too well. They would say they couldn't sell a Polaris ATV because it didn't have a shaft drive or it didn't have a manual transmission. Their loyalty was to the first brand they had. So in a short time we decided that if we were going to grow Polaris ATVs in the South, we needed to find dealers that weren't selling a competitive brand, and that seemed to work out the best for us.[10]

Going Gang Busters

By the summer of 1984, the Polaris ATVs were far enough along to make Hall Wendel declare, "We're going gang busters on the three-wheeler and four-wheeler program."[11]

On July 21, 1984, Polaris celebrated its 30th anniversary with a huge birthday bash in Roseau featuring—among other things—a community breakfast, plant tours, an air show, an autograph session, and a country music dance. Polaris founders Edgar Hetteen and David Johnson were on hand to carve the first pieces from a life-size snowmobile cake that was so realistic that more than one person mistook it for the real thing.

Early in the afternoon, crowds gathered for what promised to be one of the biggest events of the day—a series of races featuring what the company called its three-wheelers and four-wheelers.

Polaris made plans to begin production on the three- and four-wheelers the following spring. "Our dealers are asking for them," Ochs told a local reporter. "This is our number one priority right now."[12] By the end of the year, Hall Wendel was telling anyone who would listen that he was "totally confident that we have a superior machine to comparable three-wheelers and four-wheelers."[13]

In March 1985, Polaris's first-production ATVs started rolling off the assembly line accompanied by cheers in Roseau. With the introduction of the three-wheel Scrambler and the four-wheel

Below: Hall Wendel (far left) watches as David Johnson (center) and Edgar Hetteen (right) cut into the biggest (and perhaps only) snowmobile cake ever made. Roseau bakers Charles and David Honl created the 1,044-pound cake using 80 sheet cakes, each measuring 161" by 262", and more than 150 pounds of icing.

Bottom: Another cake was created for Polaris's 30th anniversary and presented to (from left) Edgar Hetteen, David Johnson, and Hall Wendel. *(Photo courtesy David Johnson.)*

Above left: Minnesota governor Rudy Perpich addresses the crowd gathered at the Roseau plant for Polaris's ATV kickoff celebration.

Above right: The first Polaris all-terrain vehicle rolls down the Roseau plant's assembly line in 1984.

Trail Boss, Polaris was finally approaching its goal of year-round employment.

As Ochs told the crowd that had gathered for the first day of production, the beginning of the ATV era marked a turning point for Polaris and for Roseau.

As we move into the manufacturing cycle of all-terrain vehicles, we are making a transition from less than 50 year-round employees to nearly 200 people employed year round. We know how important this is to all of you. The credit for this move into all-terrain vehicles rests with all of our employees. It is the result of innovation, flexibility and productivity.[14]

Shortly after those first ATV races at the 30th anniversary bash, Polaris worked with the David L. Mona pubic relations firm (later acquired by Weber Shandwick) to introduce the ATVs at a press launch. "We rented a farm south of the Twin Cities where people could ride the ATVs and brought in trade editors from around the country," said Mona.[15]

The idea was to penetrate a whole set of trade publications that were unfamiliar or only moderately familiar with Polaris. The ATVs were introduced, and then the trade editors could go out and ride them. Most of them were snowmobile enthusiasts and had never before been on an ATV. Afterwards, there were a number of cover stories on the Polaris ATVs, which gave Polaris a positive initial thrust into the new arena.[16]

Mona said the success of the press event also gave Polaris confidence that it was on the right track. Still, Polaris—a mere four years after its near extinction—was entering a market dominated by Japanese manufacturers Honda, Yamaha, Kawasaki, and Suzuki. While Hall Wendel insisted that his company had already proven "unequivocally" that it could compete with Japanese-made products, Polaris faced a daunting challenge. All of the Japanese companies had been making ATVs for at least four or five years. (Honda had actually introduced its first model in 1970.) How could Polaris break into the ATV market after getting such a late start? The answer was clear: Polaris needed to carve out a niche for itself.

Staking Out Territory

By the time the company introduced the Scrambler and the Trail Boss, the niche carving had already begun. Polaris had decided early on to market its new product as "the all-purpose ATV that works as hard as it plays."

"What we were trying to target was an adult market that was keyed into the farming and sportsman category," external relations manager Marlys Knutson said. "We would leave the recreational market for the Japanese competition."[17]

"We were looking at utility more than recreation when we introduced the ATV," said Jerry Endrizzi, production support supervisor for the ATV group. "We wanted the farmer to be able to hook it on to his pickup truck and go out to his combine. Then when he's done combining, he can ride the ATV back in rather than having to drive the combine two miles home."[18]

Polaris's market strategy based on utility led to another decision that would soon prove fortuitous. It began concentrating most of its ATV efforts on the design, production, and marketing of four-wheelers, not three-wheelers. The four-wheel Trail Bosses had proven to be more stable and to have better traction than the three-wheel Scramblers. This made them especially useful on the farm and in the workplace.

By August 1985, Polaris officials were predicting that the Trail Boss would outsell the Scrambler three to one. "The four-wheelers [are] new," said production supervisor Orvis Olson, "and anything new on the market always takes the place of its predecessor."[19] In fact, Polaris stopped making three-wheelers after that first year of production, even converting some of its three-wheelers into four-wheelers. Polaris had built about 500 three-wheelers and sold some of them, but on hearing of numerous cases in which children were being hurt on the less stable three-wheelers, Polaris bought back as many of them as it could.

In 1987 Polaris's ATV competitors also stopped selling three-wheel machines after the Consumer Product Safety Commission (CPSC) determined they were unsafe. "That CPSC decision actually turned out to be a good thing for Polaris," said Bennett Morgan, general manager for the ATV division. "The Japanese manufacturers were really hurt by it. They backed off this industry for several years, which allowed us to quickly gain a foothold against some tough competition."[20]

Safety was turning out to be a strategic marketing point. In a 1987 consent decree settlement with the government, Polaris's competitors in the ATV market agreed "to set up a national headquarters to develop training programs for ATV riders."[21] Polaris went a step further. Every Polaris ATV dealer was a certified trainer, and all buyers of Polaris ATVs would, from then on, have to complete Polaris's own specially developed training course in order to activate the warranties on their new machines. The course had two parts: a video demonstrating safe riding techniques and a hands-on riding session in which customers were required to show that they could handle the machines safely. Polaris also instituted one other safety-related policy that was unique in the industry: no sales to anyone under 18 years of age. "We wanted to distinguish ourselves and not get caught up in safety issues," Hall Wendel explained.[22]

In its first year of production, 1985, Polaris manufactured just over 9,000 ATVs. At the company's year-end profit-sharing distribution meeting, held at Roseau High School, Hall Wendel thanked the company's employees for doing what some people thought was impossible. "We were able to launch the ATV product line in half of the time originally set," he said. "This has been a tremendous achievement." Chuck Baxter told the crowd of 1,100 that the company was now gearing up to introduce a new line of "four-wheel-drive four-wheelers."[23]

Such gratitude toward employees was par for the course at Polaris. "Even when we started to become a big company, with 1,000 employees, it was still a family company," said Pam Hetteen. "Arnie Ochs and Hall Wendel instilled that feeling, and that's what made Polaris so successful."[24]

With the introduction of its ATVs, Polaris became more than a snowmobile company. For the first time in its history, it was producing a major product in numbers that rivaled its snowmobile production (although 10 years would pass before the number of ATVs surpassed the number of snowmobiles manufactured). Polaris was transforming itself, but ATVs were only one part of the transformation process.

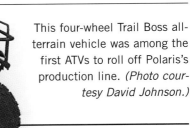

This four-wheel Trail Boss all-terrain vehicle was among the first ATVs to roll off Polaris's production line. *(Photo courtesy David Johnson.)*

DAVID JOHNSON RETIRES

FRIDAY, FEBRUARY 19, 1988, WAS David Johnson's last official day on the job at Polaris. As the day came to a close, most of the Roseau employees gathered at an appropriate location—the end of the assembly line—to wish the company's cofounder well.

Arnie Ochs summed up what most of the people there felt: "All of us here today have our jobs and have this opportunity because of David. It's never been David's style to let the spotlight shine on himself, but it is only appropriate that we let it shine on him today."[1]

Despite his retirement, Johnson never really left Polaris. He continued to be a nearly daily presence at the Roseau plant for years to come.

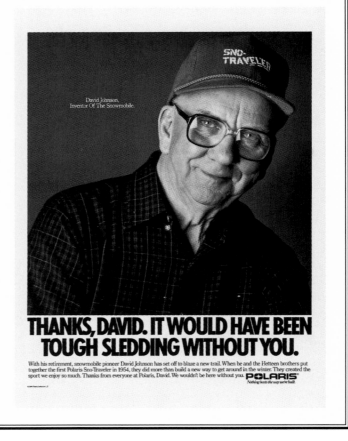

David Johnson, Inventor Of The Snowmobile.

THANKS, DAVID. IT WOULD HAVE BEEN TOUGH SLEDDING WITHOUT YOU.

With his retirement, snowmobile pioneer David Johnson has set off to blaze a new trail. When he and the Hetteen brothers put together the first Polaris Sno-Traveler in 1954, they did more than build a new way to get around in the winter. They created the sport we enjoy so much. Thanks from everyone at Polaris, David. We wouldn't be here without you. **POLARIS** *Nothing beats the way we're built.*

"All of a sudden we had a pretty viable company," said Bob Moe, "so Hall and I started looking at going public."[25]

Going Public

In October 1986, Polaris announced that it had filed with the Securities and Exchange Commission (SEC) to sell its stock on the open market. Under the plan filed with the SEC, shares for the sale would come from current stockholders, all of whom were members of the management group that had bought the company from Textron in 1981. The preliminary prospectus that accompanied the SEC filing reported that Polaris's sales had increased nearly 800 percent in the previous five years.[26]

The initial public offering, or IPO, was delayed by what Hall Wendel called "general market conditions beyond our control,"[27] but 11 months later,

the nine members of the ownership group sold 80 percent of their holdings in the company, netting more than $98 million.[28] Polaris went public, not as a corporation but as a master limited partnership (MLP)—a form of ownership under which individual investors pay taxes on company profits.

While Hall Wendel and the rest of the management group retained control over company operations, the IPO did bring several immediate changes. As an MLP, Polaris increased the amount of money it distributed to its workers through profit sharing and instituted a stock ownership plan for employees. It also became accountable to thousands of investors who expected to see the value of their shares (or, more accurately, partnership units) increase. "We feel a moral obligation to our employees, to Polaris and to the 13,000 [new] investors," Hall Wendel announced. "We have a financial incentive to continue to prosper in a successful manner and we fully intend to keep going."[29]

Polaris was now in the business of maximizing shareholder value.

Becoming a Growth Company

For years, Polaris had been looking for a new product that would let it take advantage of its unused production capacity during down times in the snowmobile manufacturing cycle. Now, with the ATVs demanding more and more time on the production line, surplus capacity was no longer the problem. Ochs explained the situation to a meeting of Polaris employees in December 1985.

The output, the capacity of the . . . system is limited, so we are in the midst of evaluating how we should operate the plant, whether we need two assembly lines, whether we should run lot production, or whether we should try to run staggered, one ATV and one snowmobile. . . . There are a lot of cost implications and it takes a great deal of study and much evaluation to assess the most effective way to do it. We hope to have that complete and a direction established early in 1986 so we will have extended capabilities for future years.[30]

Seven months later, Polaris broke ground on the largest expansion in its history, a $3 million, 68,500-square-foot addition to the Roseau plant. "This expansion will allow us to increase our output and improve our product quality and efficiencies," Hall Wendel declared.[31] In April 1987, snowmobile production began in the newly completed addition. The factory now boasted two production lines. Parts whisked through a new, $1.3 million paint system, emerging cleaned, painted, and baked in just 65 minutes.[32]

Around the same time, Polaris began flexing its growing muscles—with mixed results.

First it filed a complaint with the federal government's International Trade Commission (ITC) alleging Japanese ATV makers were dumping their machines on the U.S. market at prices below the cost of production. Although the ITC eventually ruled against Polaris, the Japanese companies responded by dramatically raising their prices. "So while we lost the battle, we won the war," said Bob Nygaard.[33]

Polaris president Ken Larson oversaw a period of controlled expansion and diversification during the 1980s and 1990s.

Then Polaris made a well-publicized offer to acquire its rival, Arctco, the maker of Arctic Cat snowmobiles. "If a marriage were to take place, it is our feeling it would be to the benefit of all concerned," Hall Wendel said in announcing the offer. Arctco turned Wendel down and instead sold one-third of its stock to Suzuki.

Finally, in late 1988, Polaris made a big change at the top, bringing in a former Toro executive, Ken Larson, to become the company's new president and chief operating officer. Larson had gained a reputation at Toro as a corporate "hit man" who excelled at trimming corporate fat. While Larson did make substantial cuts to Polaris's workforce in the months after his arrival, he quickly concluded that Polaris needed to readjust its "lean and mean" attitude. It had to learn how to become the kind of growth company that investors loved.

I was in a situation where I could come on board and say "Okay, everything that's been done so far is great, but it's time for some major transitions, in terms of capacity." We had done a great job of utilizing the capacity we had and controlling overhead and continuing to build on it, therefore becoming very profitable. But we didn't have much of anything left. If we were going to keep growing, we had to do something dramatically different. We had to start expanding. . . . We needed to move from battening down the hatches to an environment of controlled growth.[34]

Hall Wendel also replaced his father as CEO and ushered in a new phase in Polaris's evolution.

"It was an exciting era with Hall Wendel at the helm," said Ed Skomoroh. "Hall often shot from the hip, but he was damn accurate most of the time."[35]

The 1990 Indy RXL was the industry's first electronically fuel injected (EFI) snowmobile. Polaris workers in Roseau worked under a tight deadline to make sure the machine qualified for the 1989–1990 racing season. *(Photo courtesy* Snow Goer Magazine.*)*

"When Hall took over, that was the start of a new culture at Polaris," said Marlys Olsen, who was hired in 1966 and later became supervisor of brakes and struts. "I remember having a picnic outside between the two buildings [in Roseau], and Hall gave a speech about how he was here to be part of Roseau, that good things were coming."[36]

Good things were indeed coming. In the first five years of his tenure, Larson oversaw a series of expansions and improvements to meet growing demand for Polaris products. The company added two production lines at the Roseau plant (in 1991 and 1993), introduced robotic welders, and bought Northern Metals Specialties, a metal fabrication company in Osceola, Wisconsin.

Prior to the improvements initiated by Larson, Jeff Bjorkman, vice president of operations, explained that Polaris was "trying to do everything. We were doing fabrication, making our own decals, our own seats. We were doing just about everything possible, but it was very high cost to do it that way. There were too many irons in the fire, and material flow was atrocious."[37]

Polaris's new commitment to "controlled growth" appealed to investors while helping the company accommodate and encourage the innovative spirit that had always thrived within its walls. As it happened, Ken Larson's arrival coincided with a flurry of product innovations that propelled the company into a decade of unprecedented growth.

One of these innovations was the Big Boss offroad 6x6, introduced in 1989 with automatic transmission and a hinged cargo bed that could haul up to 650 (later 800) pounds. The six-wheel-drive Big Boss had the maneuverability of an ATV but could still haul tremendous loads. One magazine called it a "monster machine [that] is a crossbreed with ATV features and utility vehicle cargo capabilities."[38]

"The Big Boss 6x6 was in a class of its own," said Ed Skomoroh. "It was never copied by the competition."[39]

Over the years, the Big Boss's unique features proved valuable in a number of ways. In 1991, for example, Polaris supplied the U.S. Marine Corps with a few Big Bosses for some "electronic snooping," according to Chuck Baxter. Dubbed "Robo-Spies" by the *Wall Street Journal*, the Big Bosses were modified by the military to hold a night-vision video camera and electronics to make them operable by remote control.[40] Later, during the record Red River Flood of 1997, Polaris employees would use five Big Bosses to transport hundreds of tons of sandbags to otherwise inaccessible areas in Minnesota and North Dakota to help staunch the dangerous floodwaters.

Better Sleds

Even with the growing prominence of its ATV line, Polaris was still primarily a snowmobile company. Throughout the late 1980s, snowmobiles rolled out at twice the rate of ATVs. On the income side, snowmobiles accounted for more than two-thirds of the company's total sales. In 1990 the national press reported that Polaris had finally pulled ahead of competitors Arctic Cat, Yamaha, and Bombardier to claim the largest slice of the snowmobile market—about 30 percent.[41]

For several years after Polaris had cemented the number one position in worldwide snowmobile sales, "We kept the humble, small company position by not mentioning it to the press or in our brochures," said Ed Skomoroh. "Then one day we said, 'Hey, why not? We beat out the Japanese snowmobile manufacturer [Yamaha] and the snowmobile company from Canada [Bombardier], and the other Minnesota snowmobile company [Arctic Cat]. Let's not brag, but let's tell the users who the real leader is.' So we started talking about our being leaders in technology, innovation, styling, suspension, and engines. And then we'd say, 'And by the way, we're number one in sales.'"[42]

Polaris intended to maintain its snowmobile momentum, said Skomoroh, by continuing to create "new niches, new concepts, new performance models . . . based on strong, proven technology, not something brand new that hasn't been tested."[43]

The new concepts came fast and furious.

In 1989 Polaris broke new ground when it introduced the industry's first electronically fuel injected (EFI) snowmobile. The Indy 650 RXL was a seriously fast machine, recommended for "experienced riders only."

"It's got the same size engine as some small cars," marveled production supervisor Bob Welin.

Crates of new 1985 Indy 600s
await shipment from the Roseau plant.

Under International Snowmobile Racing (ISR) rules, the RXLs would be eligible for the upcoming racing season only if their assembly was completed by December 1. During three days at the end of November, a crew of about 240 Polaris employees worked around the clock to crank out 500 of the new machines and beat the deadline.

Although Polaris received a slew of positive reviews about its EFI breakthrough, news coverage took a negative turn the following summer. In June 1990, a company called Injection Research Specialists filed a trade-secret lawsuit claiming that Polaris and Polaris's engine maker, Fuji Heavy Industries, had misappropriated its EFI technology. Eight years later, Polaris and Fuji would reach an agreement with Injection Research to settle all outstanding claims.[44]

The 1990–1991 season featured another new line of machines that helped strengthen the company's position in what it called the "economy class" of the snowmobile market. Consumers had been hoping for years—ever since the introduction of the

first Indys in the early 1980s—that Polaris would produce a low-cost sled with independent front suspension (IFS). Polaris knew it was a good idea. ("If you could combine the two, IFS and great price, you'd have another winner," said Bob Nygaard).[45] But that combination had proven elusive. The engineering group had trouble thinking of Indys as anything other than high-performance machines. "They would take a design, drive it, and say, 'This is not an Indy,'" recalled Skomoroh. "We said, 'No, it's not an Indy. It's for the person who buys a [Yamaha] Bravo or a [Ski-Doo] Elan or a [Yamaha] Enticer.'"[46]

Finally, after years of work, Polaris came up with the right combination and in 1990 introduced the Indy Lite and the Indy StarLite—two machines that bundled IFS technology into low-cost packages. Both models sold out before the snow even hit the ground. "Polaris dealers were hot for these models," Skomoroh proclaimed a few months after their introduction.[47]

That spring, the company reported that the two machines had helped quadruple its sales in the economy class. "The intent of the Indy Lite was to spread the independent front suspension throughout the snowmobile line and still have extremely attractive pricing," Chuck Baxter said. "It's been successful."[48]

The other big snowmobile innovation of this period was the Indy XLT—the successor to Polaris's ultrasuccessful Indy 500. The discussions over how to upgrade the Indy 500 had split the company into two camps: one that wanted to simply increase displacement and performance of the existing 488 cc twin-cylinder engine and one that preferred to go with a new, three-cylinder engine—assuming it was possible to build a triple without adding too much weight.

The discussion went on for weeks and culminated when Bob Nygaard and one of the company's most talented engineers, Jan Hedlund, were having dinner at the Roseau Dairy Queen. "I can remember Jan sketching out a rudimentary design for the three-cylinder XLT motor on a napkin," Nygaard recalled. "That led to even further discussions."[49] It took a few months, but Polaris and its engine builders at Fuji eventually came up with a three-cylinder design that was both light and affordable.

XLT stood for "Extra Light Triple" and was a classic case of naming by committee, said Nygaard.

We didn't know what to call it. Ken Larson, Ed Skomoroh, and I came up with the name while we were coming back on a plane one night. We knew that weight was an issue with a three-cylinder motor, so we each chose a word to indicate that this was a lightweight triple-cylinder engine. I think I chose "extra," or "X," and Ken chose "light," or "L," and Ed chose "triple," or "T." That's where XLT came from.[50]

Polaris introduced the Indy XLT for the 1992–1993 model year, and the new machine accounted for nearly one-third of the almost 50,000 sleds the company built that season.[51] "It was an absolute home run," Nygaard said, "just a runaway success."[52]

That success was shortly followed by another triumph in 1994 when Polaris introduced two new sleds for model year 1995: the XLT Special and the RXL, both of which featured the snowmobile industry's first OEM (original equipment manufac-ture) long-travel rear suspension. The groundbreaking engineering was so successful that most of Polaris's subsequent snowmobile models also featured long-travel rear suspension.

The long-travel rear suspension, Nygaard explained, "provided a better ride by having more suspension travel, and it was also a coupled design. Coupling allows the front and the rear of the rear suspension to communicate with each other. As the magazines characterized it, this was the biggest improvement in snowmobile ride and handling since Polaris introduced independent front suspension."[53]

Without a doubt, the trade magazine editors valued Polaris's latest engineering innovation; the 1995 XLT Special became *Snow Goer Magazine*'s "Sled of the Year."

Making a Splash

Polaris did not limit its innovative energies to snowmobiles or, for that matter, ATVs. The late

The Indy XLT in action. Polaris engineer Jan Hedlund sketched the design for the 1993 Indy XLT's groundbreaking three-cylinder engine on a Dairy Queen napkin. *(Photo courtesy* Snow Goer Magazine.*)*

Polaris's first attempts to develop a personal watercraft produced little success, but that had all changed by 1991. *(Photo courtesy David Johnson.)*

1980s and early 1990s were the formative years of yet another new product that would strengthen the company through diversification. Polaris was preparing to dive into the choppy waters of personal watercraft (PWC).

With a full line of top-selling snowmobiles and a growing stable of ATVs, Polaris was more diversified than it had ever been—but not diversified enough to satisfy Hall Wendel, Bob Moe, and Polaris's new president, Ken Larson. The ATV market had weakened considerably in the first few years after Polaris introduced its three- and four-wheelers, and the ATV itself was proving to be, at this early point in its existence, a seasonal product much like the snowmobile. While the company remained bullish on the ATV's future, it was still looking for another product to help it diversify.

Polaris found what it was looking for on the water. In the words of Chuck Baxter, "We were watching some of our competitors work on personal watercraft. . . . We started really getting more serious when some of our competitors started doing it."[54]

Personal watercraft—described by *Forbes* magazine as "$3,000 to $6,000 water skis with handles and motors [that] shoot across the water at speeds of up to 40 miles an hour"—were just

beginning, in the late 1980s, to make a dent in the ailing marine industry. Kawasaki's Jet Ski stand-up watercraft dominated the market, but newer, sit-down models manufactured by Yamaha, Bombardier, and several smaller firms were starting to catch on. This budding market, wrote *Forbes*, seemed "just right" for Polaris. Hall Wendel agreed. "It's a natural fit to what we already do," he told *Forbes*. "It uses a similar engine, and it can go through our existing distribution channels."[55]

Polaris made no secret of its plans to enter the PWC market. In December 1988, Chuck Baxter told a meeting of hundreds of Polaris employees that the company might introduce its first PWC as early as 1990.[56] In January 1990, Clayton Carlson, then manager of manufacturing engineering, told members of the Roseau Civic and Commerce Association that Polaris planned to test a two-person "wet bike" in 1991 and hoped to go into production in 1992. "We are watching for potential legislation that could impact the design, manufacture, and utilization of this product," he said.[57]

Behind the scenes, the members of Polaris's PWC development group were learning everything they could about the competition's machines. "We had different people experimenting with them," recalled Baxter. "Eventually we came to realize that this was something that we could probably do."

It didn't take long for the Polaris team to decide that Bombardier's "Sea-Doo," not the Kawasaki Jet Ski, was the machine to beat. "We knew pretty quickly we wanted to go sit-down and not stand-up," recalled Bob Nygaard.

The question was what to do next?

By this time, Hall Wendel, who had been slow to embrace the PWC concept, decided Polaris should jump into the market and gave the green light for Polaris to produce a machine on its own.[58]

Polaris unveiled its new personal watercraft at a boat show in Chicago in September 1991. The SL650 was a two-person, sit-down craft with a powerful 650 cc triple-cylinder engine. Its hull was wider and longer than those on competing machines, which made it more reliable and stable and easier to reboard in deep water. "At the time, I was in my forties," joked Baxter, "and we designed it specifically for an overweight 45-year-old."[59]

Hall Wendel touted Polaris's new product as a perfect match between company and machine.

Our company is known for engineering excellence and high-performing, durable recreation and utility machines. The SL650 is a natural extension of this product mix—we're taking advantage of our strengths to develop a machine for a market where we can see a significant growth opportunity. . . . There's great product synergy here. Customers associate the Polaris name with quality, performance, and durability. Plus, our dealers know service and know our machines inside and out.[60]

The PWC became the third leg of Polaris's product stool. "And it was not just the third leg on the stool for us," said Bob Nygaard. "It was a third leg on the stool for dealers. It gave them another product to sell counter to snowmobiles, and it could increase our penetration in the South and in the California markets." On the day Polaris introduced the watercraft, a dealer shook Nygaard's hand and thanked him for just having "put my kids through college."[61]

Mitchell Johnson, son of Polaris founder David Johnson, nephew of Polaris founder Edgar Hetteen, and once manager of the PWC engineering team, saw the SL650's introduction as yet another example of how Polaris people responded to a challenge.

How do you take these people who are building some of the finest snowmobiles in the world, turn around and take on the Japanese and build some of the finest ATVs in the world, and turn around and do it again on boats? These people, many of them, grew up here in Roseau—they didn't come from boat hull manufacturing companies or ATV manufacturing companies. They just say "Let's do it." You take some of our best snowmobile suspension guys, put them on a boat hull, and say we

have to make a boat hull that'll work better than anyone else's. And they do it.[62]

By this time, three companies—Kawasaki, Yamaha, and Bombardier—dominated the PWC market, accounting for about 95 percent of total sales. As it had when it entered the ATV market six years earlier, Polaris was betting that its name recognition and reputation for making high-quality, high-performance machines would help it gain a foothold in what appeared to be a crowded industry. Hall Wendel expressed confidence that the company's PWC operation would turn a profit soon after starting up.[63]

Polaris manufactured nearly 7,000 PWCs during the first year of production in 1992, and almost all those machines were snapped up soon after hitting the sales floor. "We really had instant demand," Ed Skomoroh recalled.[64]

The following year, the company introduced a new, more powerful model, the SL750, and increased production by more than 50 percent. Ken Larson was predicting big things for the new machine.[65] Others at the company were equally gung ho on the PWC. "It was really good," Baxter said. "At the time, it was probably the best one on the market."[66]

In February 1993, when Polaris released its annual report for the previous year, the sales figures graphically illustrated how quickly the company was changing. ATVs now accounted for one quarter of Polaris sales. The new PWCs accounted for a respectable 7 percent, while parts, clothing, and accessories represented 14 percent. Snowmobiles still claimed a little more than half the sales pie, but the trend was clear: the non-snowmobile product lines were quickly gaining ground. In fact, 1992 would be the last year in which Polaris was, in sales terms, mainly a snowmobile company.

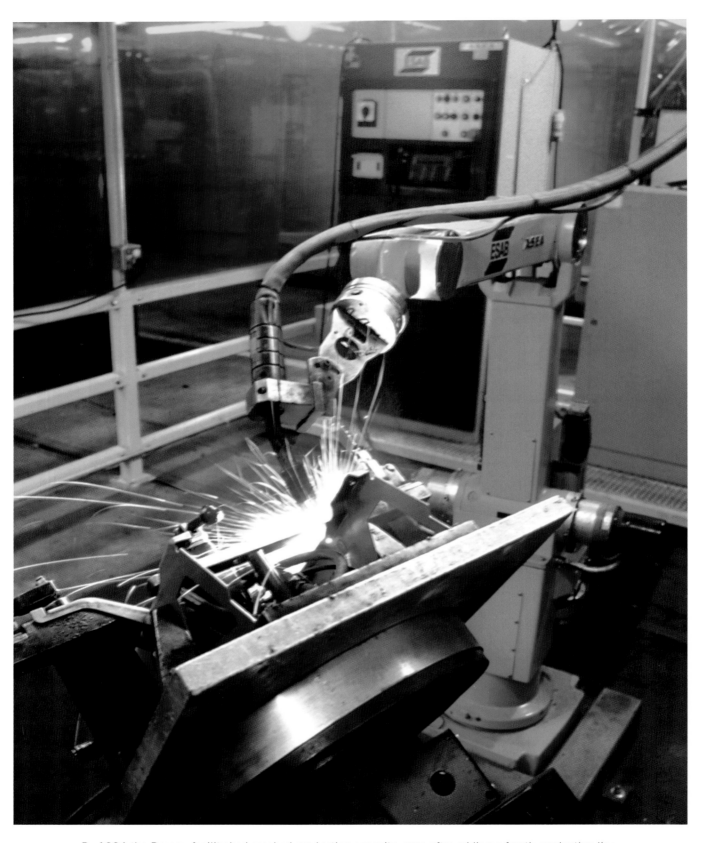

By 1994 the Roseau facility had reached production capacity, even after adding a fourth production line.

CHAPTER NINE

A NEW KIND OF COMPANY

1994–1996

For all our success in the snowmobile industry, Polaris today is much more than just a snowmobile company.

—Polaris Industries Inc. 1996 Annual Report

PAM HETTEEN WASN'T SURE how many people would show up in Roseau for Polaris's 40th birthday party during the last weekend of July 1994. Excitement had been building for several weeks: People were scrambling to put the finishing touches on their parade floats. Employees were shining up the plant to impress the expected throngs of visitors. Polaris aficionados from all over North America—including two groups of Polaris dealers who wanted to travel to Roseau on personal watercraft—were making plans to join the festivities. As cochairperson for the event (along with Marlys Knutson, who led the event team), Pam Hetteen suspected that it would be a big party. She just didn't know how big.

By Friday night, more than 6,000 people had registered to take part in the weekend's activities. The following morning, the local Lion's Club served about 3,200 breakfasts to visitors at the Polaris plant. In all, an estimated 15,000 people descended on the little town of 2,500. They shuttled from event to event and lined the streets for what was billed as the largest parade in Roseau's history. "It was extremely successful," Pam Hetteen declared. "I received so many comments about how totally amazed everyone was with the party and how everything was free."[1]

The people of Roseau could not help but get caught up in the excitement. "Does [Polaris] have an impact on Roseau and surrounding area?" Mayor Bernie Burggraf asked readers of the *Roseau Times-Region.* "You betchur boots!"[2] Small businesses in the area went out of their way to link themselves to the town's biggest employer. "We Salute Polaris And Their Employees For Choosing Roseau For 40 Years!" proclaimed a half-page ad for Wally's supermarket. "Thank you for all the GREAT products!" enthused the folks at D&E Sports. Polaris workers joined in the chorus, too. "All days are good ones," insisted longtime employee and retired snowmobile racer Randy Hites. "I still like working here. Everything that I have, Polaris bought for me."

It seemed to many people who attended the big birthday bash that the relationship between Polaris and Roseau was stronger than ever. The relationship, however, was already going through some major changes.

Iowa Bound

The month before, in June 1994, Polaris had announced that it was moving its entire PWC production to a vacant factory in Spirit Lake,

Thousands of people showed up in Roseau to help Polaris celebrate its 40th anniversary in July 1994.

Above: Sno-Travelers and other vintage Polaris snowmobiles drew cheers from the crowd during what was billed as the biggest parade in Roseau's history.

Right: A parade of Polaris personal watercraft rode up the Roseau River to kick off the company's 40th anniversary celebration.

Iowa, just south of the Minnesota border. For the first time in its history, Polaris was opening a major manufacturing operation somewhere other than Roseau.

The news hit Roseau's business and community leaders hard. Was this a sign of things to come? A local bank president asked vice president of manufacturing Jim Bruha why Polaris couldn't just hire more workers in the area.

"Because they just aren't there," Bruha replied. "Some people just don't want to live in northern Minnesota."

Bruha explained further that Polaris had decided to make the move because the company was expanding and the Roseau area could no longer supply the extra workers that the company needed. In fact, the company had recently been forced to put 26 people from engineering on the production line just to keep it running. Polaris had looked long and hard at expanding the Roseau facility, Bruha said. "It just won't work."

Rumors started spreading around town that Polaris was getting ready to abandon Roseau, but Polaris officials moved quickly to dampen that speculation. As evidence of their continued commitment to Roseau, they pointed to the recent addition of a fourth production line, dedicated to

ATVs, at the Roseau facility. "We are not downsizing Roseau," Bruha insisted. "We will continue to see some increase in growth in Roseau, just not at the 15, 20, or 40 percent rate we've witnessed recently."[3]

Before long, even those who had been most alarmed began to acknowledge that Polaris's expansion to Iowa made sense. "Electrical supplies, water lines, sanitary sewers, streets and affordable housing units just have not kept up with the growth potential of Roseau's number one industry," a local columnist wrote.[4] "If a worker wants to come to Roseau and work at Polaris, he or she will have to sleep in a tent in the park because housing that's affordable for entry level Polaris workers doesn't exist in Roseau."[5]

Unlike Roseau, Spirit Lake, Iowa, had a surplus of potential workers and an empty manufacturing plant. In addition, its location offered potential freight and distribution savings given the large number of PWCs sold in the southern United States. "There is some attractiveness in being further south," Ken Larson said. "We can do more [watercraft] testing early in the spring and later in the fall."[6]

In addition, Spirit Lake was a community that fit Polaris's can-do culture. "Small-town-wise, it has a lot of things that Roseau has—a strong identification between the business and the community, a lot of community pride, a great education system," said Chuck Crone, the first plant manager for the Spirit Lake facility, who later became Polaris's first director of purchasing. "Because it's a recreation area, the people identify with Polaris products. So culturally, before we went there, we thought it would be a pretty good fit."[7]

When Crone arrived at the new plant on August 15, 1994, the building was completely empty except for "a leftover desk, a chair, and a telephone," he said. He supervised the installation of the first of three new PWC production lines and the hiring of more than 100 employees (from a pool of more than 1,000 applicants).

In only seven weeks, Polaris had done what an outsider might have deemed impossible. The company had turned an empty facility into a functioning plant. As LaRae Krahn, human resources manager for Roseau's engineering group, pointed out, "We [at Polaris] believe there's nothing we can't do. We had production lines up and running so soon because we didn't think we couldn't do it."[8]

Production was ready to roll at the beginning of October even though, as Chuck Crone recalled, some of the new hires weren't convinced *they* were ready.

I had these 20 new people in the office, and I called them in the Friday before the production people were coming in and told them the coming Monday was kind of a big day, that if everybody went around acting like they were new, we'd have chaos. I said, "I know you're new, but you can't be telling these people you're new. As far as they're concerned, you've been here all your life. When we

start on Monday, it's okay not to know something, but don't ever say 'I'm new.' Say 'I don't know.' Come into the office. We'll find the answer out, and we'll go back out and tell them what the answer is." So from that, the staff at Spirit Lake actually set in motion a kind of tradition: When we hire a new person, they can be new for only a day.[9]

At the plant's official opening ceremonies in November, Polaris officials expressed their delight with the new facility and its employees. "We couldn't be happier here," Ken Larson declared. "The opening of this plant means the beginning of a brand-new chapter for Polaris."[10]

This "brand-new chapter" bespoke a new corporate vision that increasingly looked beyond Roseau to accommodate the growing company.

In 1994 Polaris moved its entire PWC production from the Roseau facility (pictured) to a new plant in Spirit Lake, Iowa.

Expanding Horizons

On December 22, 1994, Polaris officially became a publicly traded corporation. The company had operated as a master limited partnership (MLP) since 1987, but now, with the overwhelming support of its unit holders,

the company was converting itself into a publicly traded corporation. Under existing tax laws, if Polaris entered "a substantially new line of business," it risked losing certain tax benefits it had enjoyed as an MLP.

Polaris's senior management team—including Hall Wendel, who owned more than 5 percent of the outstanding units—felt the time was right to make the switch. "The company decided to undertake the conversion now," Wendel explained, "so that Polaris could maximize value for shareholders and broaden the potential market for Polaris stock with mutual funds, pensions, and other institutional investors. The conversion also will enable Polaris to aggressively build its business by developing or acquiring new product lines."[11]

Six weeks later, in February 1995, Polaris Industries Inc. began to "aggressively build its business" when it announced a joint venture with its longtime partner Fuji Heavy Industries to manufacture small engines at a new plant in Hudson, Wisconsin. Polaris would own 40 percent of the new company, called Robin Manufacturing USA, and Fuji would own the remaining 60 percent. Plans called for the Robin plant to build engines for Polaris ATVs and Textron E-Z-Go golf carts.

The move, said Ken Larson, would help Polaris cope with U.S.-Japanese currency fluctuations.

"The major reason for doing this is to build for the long term, to position [Polaris] so the exchange rate between the dollar and the yen would have a lot less impact."[12]

Polaris Starts Its Engine

In early August 1995, Polaris made another big move in Wisconsin when it purchased a manufacturing facility adjacent to its existing fabrication plant in Osceola. "With continued strong demand for snowmobiles, personal watercraft, and all-terrain vehicles, we need room to grow," Hall Wendel explained.[13]

Wendel did not say what the company's exact plans were for the new Osceola facility. Those plans were not made public until October, when Polaris announced that it would soon begin manufacturing its own watercraft engines in Osceola. "The goal is to have three sources for our engines for all our products," Wendel said, "Fuji, Robin, and our own production models."[14]

Development of the Polaris-designed watercraft engines had been in the works for some time. It all started when Martin Heinrich, a 20-year engine design veteran at Kohler Company, began working for Polaris in 1991. "I had engines in my blood," he said. "When I came to Polaris, I thought it would be a good idea for us to have our own engine. Management was a little insecure about the idea, but I eventually talked to Chuck Baxter, my boss, and he gave me the go-ahead."[15]

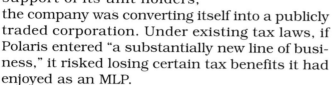

Above: In 1994, chairman and CEO Hall Wendel, an avid mountain climber, became the 24th person ever to "summit" the tallest peaks of all seven continents when he reached the top of Mount Everest.

Right: In the 1990s, Bob Moe (left), Ken Larson (center), and Hall Wendel became familiar faces to investors after Polaris became a publicly traded corporation.

Jeff Bjorkman, vice president of operations, explained why Polaris felt it needed to design and manufacture its own engines. "Fuji's parent company was having financial problems, so they were underinvesting in R&D," he said. "We had some quality issues and technology issues as the industry was changing. Performance levels were rising, and we weren't satisfied that we were getting the investment in Fuji's business to get us where we had to be in engine technology."[16]

Still, Polaris had good reason to be cautious when it came to designing its own engine. Heinrich, as manager of engine design and development, was the only man at Polaris who had any kind of formal experience in designing engines. The company had no engine department, only a development group that tested engines.

Heinrich and his small engine group went to work and soon came up with drawings of the design. Management, still skeptical, sent the drawings to Fuji Heavy Industries to solicit its expertise.

"Fuji said the engine couldn't be assembled," said Heinrich. "They said it wouldn't even turn over. Our design team just laughed, but our managers, of course, were a little bit insecure."[17]

Using a set of hand tools, Heinrich and his team put the engine together on the floor of an office at the Osceola facility. "It was a primitive thing," remembered Heinrich.

The Osceola plant manager came in and asked, "Well, does it turn over?" I said, "Yeah, of course it turns over." So we went to Ken Larson and said, "Hey, Ken, it turns over." So then we put the pistons and cylinders on. We torqued everything down. We had compression. We checked for spark, and the spark was okay. We hooked up the starter, and we carried the engine outside on the lawn in front of the building and held it down with some two-by-fours. Then we hooked up the gas, and I can still see the gasoline running through the transparent line. As soon as the gas hit the carburetor, the engine fired up, and we revved it up.[18]

The small group of designers gave off a cheer. The plant manager ran back inside to call Hall Wendel. "The guys got all excited," said Heinrich. "It's always a really exciting moment when the engine goes on the dyno [dynamometer] and makes its first sound."[19]

A year later, Heinrich and his engine group came out with the snowmobile version. Both designs proved extremely successful, and by September 2001, Polaris was manufacturing some of its own ATV engines as well.

Polaris's decision to manufacture its own engines was, in the words of Jeff Bjorkman, "the biggest leap we've made as a company."

There was a lot of skepticism, but we had the right people on the job, people who knew what was important in the design. And we had the right supply partners who would help us through the things that we didn't know. We hired some people who had manufacturing experience in engines to help us design the end-line testing systems to make sure we did it right. And we've had great success.[20]

In addition to giving the company more protection against the fluctuating yen, Polaris's new engine-making capability offered a new marketing opportunity. It could now tag some of its products with the "Made in the USA" label, something that its competitors were unable to do.[21]

Another Border Crossing

In the summer of 1996, Polaris followed up its expansions into Iowa and Wisconsin by breaking ground on a new parts, clothing, and accessories distribution center in Vermillion, South Dakota, called the Vermillion Worldwide Distribution Center. The 250,000-square-foot facility with 30 feet of height clearance was designed to replace the company's warehousing operations in two Minneapolis-area locations. Once again, Polaris had run out of space. "We've had exceptional growth in the past few years," explained Ken Larson, "and our new facility will give us the space we need now, plus room to expand to 400,000 square feet in the future."[22]

The company had considered 135 communities throughout the upper Midwest and decided Vermillion was the best fit. Larson chose Vermillion because it offered an available workforce and an easily accessible location along Interstate 29, just south of Interstate 90.

"It's a highly automated facility, highly productive," said Bennett Morgan, who led the company's move into Vermillion. "We can ship well over $1 million worth of parts and accessories each day from that facility, and our service levels have dramatically improved because it's so high tech and because we have a great labor pool there—people with great farming-type work ethics."[23]

Polaris had expanded into three of the four states bordering Minnesota. Throughout the process, the company's senior managers regularly went out of their way to assure people that Polaris wasn't "running away from Minnesota."[24] Still, it was clear to anyone who paid attention that Polaris was no longer a small-town company with small-town aspirations. It was now a publicly traded corporation, answerable to thousands of shareholders, and as such, it had to grow. In 1993 the company's annual sales had topped half a billion dollars for the first time. Only two years later, sales broke the $1 billion mark. The expansion beyond Roseau was one manifestation of this incredible growth. The evolution of its product mix was another.

"Hitting the $1 billion mark was a huge milestone," Wendel said. "When we bought the company in 1981, never in our wildest, craziest dreams did we contemplate getting anywhere close to a billion dollars. Our objective back then was just to survive. So when we did hit a billion, it was a huge deal."[25]

"We didn't quite believe we'd done it," added Marlys Knutson. "But at the same time, we didn't make a big deal out of it to the public. That's just how we operated."[26]

"The can-do spirit, the integrity, honesty, and hard work—all of that didn't change," Wendel said.[27]

"On the other hand," Skomoroh said, "we realized we could no longer run Polaris like a small Minnesota company."[28]

Marlys Knutson and her crew organized a small after-work celebration at an old saloon called The Country House, where Polaris executives and distributors sipped from champagne glasses with

"Thanks a Billion" written on them. "We had a nice group of people," Wendel said. "We invited people in the trades and good customers and suppliers."[29]

But overall, Skomoroh said, the celebration was very low key. "We had a few drinks and went home to prepare for the next day," he said.[30]

Though hitting the billion-dollar milestone was certainly enough to give any company bragging rights—especially one that had been close to going under only 14 years earlier—Polaris's management remained modest. They still had a company to run, after all.

Bread and Butter

Each year the Roseau Civic and Commerce Association (called the "C and C") held a banquet. The highlight of the banquet was usually the Polaris presentation, in which a company executive would stand in front of the packed dining hall and summarize the previous year's events.

The C and C banquet on January 15, 1996, at the Roseau VFW Club was no different. Polaris's designated toastmaster, Mitchell Johnson, began his presentation with the obligatory self-deprecating remark. "When I was asked by Chuck Baxter to speak on behalf of Polaris for this banquet tonight, it didn't take long to say yes," he said. "Chuck is my boss." Johnson showed a video featuring new Polaris products, then walked his audience through a summary of the company's operations. After that, it was time for a story.

"In August, some of us had a party during our coffee break where bread and butter was served," Johnson began. He went on to explain that Polaris had always considered the snowmobile its "bread and butter," and that he had initially been disappointed when Wendel put him in charge of ATV engineering instead of snowmobile engineering.

Polaris broke ground for its new Vermillion, South Dakota, parts and accessories distribution center in the summer of 1996.

But now, Johnson said, the pecking order was changing. Total ATV sales were approaching total snowmobile sales (ATVs had already surpassed snowmobiles in terms of net margin), and the company expected, for the first time, to produce more ATVs than snowmobiles in 1996.

Then came the big punch line. "So, in honor of this progress," Johnson said, referring to the company's ATV line, "I'd like to serve Chuck Baxter, my boss, some bread and butter."[31]

Johnson handed the smiling Baxter a slice of buttered bread, and the room burst into applause. Most of the audience that night probably didn't realize how apt Johnson's punch line really was.

Competition had been growing between Polaris's "snowmobile people" and its "ATV people" ever since the company introduced ATVs in 1985. Some of its biggest snowmobile boosters found it hard to imagine that ATVs could ever challenge the snowmobile's supremacy. Marlys Knutson recalled a conversation she had in the early 1990s with two such true believers.

I was sitting in a room with a couple of our early direct-sales guys one night, and they said, "You know, why don't we just dump the ATVs and sell more snowmobiles? We can sell every one of those that we're making." I said, "Someday, you're going to eat those words." Sure enough, about three years later we were selling more ATVs than snowmobiles.[32]

In 1996, the year of Mitchell Johnson's "bread and butter" presentation, Polaris's ATV sales finally caught up with its snowmobile sales. In its annual report for that year, the snowmobile's status relative to the company's other product lines was one of the first issues addressed.

For all our success in the snowmobile industry, Polaris today is much more than just a snowmobile company. Snowmobiles represented 60 percent of sales in 1991 and now represent 37 percent. ATVs have grown from 25 percent to 37 percent, and PWCs represent 15 percent—from zero six years ago. With this year's record results, we've demonstrated again the value of the balance achieved in our business through diversification into new prod-

uct areas and the steady introduction of new models. Polaris expects diversification to continue.[33]

The quest for new products and new models of existing products became a constant theme in the company's communication with employees and the investing community. Polaris announced in May 1996 that it was reorganizing itself into separate business units for each of its major products: snowmobiles, all-terrain vehicles, and personal watercraft. "This reorganization lets us put together teams dedicated to each product line," Ed Skomoroh announced. "By decentralizing the decision making and accountability, we will improve product quality and profitability, and continue the great growth we've experienced."[34]

In 1995 Polaris had introduced the Sportsman 500 4x4 ATV, which featured another Polaris innovation: independent rear suspension rather than a straight axle, which made for a much smoother ride and provided 11 inches of ground clearance, the best in the industry. *ATV Magazine* named the Sportsman 500 the "ATV of the Year" for 1995, and the Sportsman quickly became the industry standard in power, strength, and smoothness of ride and the world's best-selling automatic transmission ATV. Kevin Mollett, senior marketing communications manager for the ATV division, observed that the Sportsman had become "a brand within a brand. . . . The Sportsman brand sells like hotcakes."[35]

In 1996 the company unveiled two new ATV models, the Xplorer 500 and the Scrambler 500, and a new diesel-powered ATV. The new machines represented Polaris's "commitment to aggressive and innovative product development . . . that brings new customers into the market and encourages repeat and trade-up business from existing customers," Hall Wendel declared.[36]

But these were not the only new products that Polaris was developing. Careful readers of the company's 1996 annual report noticed a tiny photograph toward the bottom of one of the middle pages, a photo of what looked like a boxy chunk of rock. On closer inspection, the photo turned out to be a mystery item covered in a grayish sheet. The accompanying text informed investors that "Polaris plans to unveil a completely new product line in 1997."[37]

Edgar Hetteen (front, center left) and David Johnson (front, center right), the two surviving cofounders of Polaris, lead a cheer among Polaris employees at the Roseau plant.

CHAPTER TEN

HARD TO IGNORE

1997–2002

Understand the riding experience. Live the riding experience. Work to make it better.

—Polaris's Three Commandments

P OLARIS SEEMED TO BE FLY-ing high as 1997 got under way. It had just recorded its eighth straight year of record profits. Its workforce now topped 2,300. And its products consistently received high marks from consumers and reviewers. But there was one nagging problem: Wall Street didn't seem to notice.

Polaris's stock price was stuck in the doldrums, fluctuating throughout 1996 from a high of approximately $35 to a low of $20. Polaris officials believed that the price per share—even at its height—"didn't reflect the true value of the company."[1] *Forbes* magazine, taking note of the situation, reported that Polaris's stock had "gone nowhere in the past three years."[2]

In response, the company's board of directors substantially expanded a new share-repurchase program in early 1997 in hopes of coaxing the stock price upward (and kept expanding the program into the next century). But no one expected the repurchase plan, by itself, to fix Polaris's image problem among investors. Clearly the company needed to enhance its profile on Wall Street—and what better way than to introduce a new product that would be virtually impossible to ignore.

A New Motorcycle

The genesis of Polaris's big new gamble had occurred four years earlier, in early 1993. Hall

Wendel, flush with the optimism generated by the introduction of the company's first personal watercraft, was eager to continue rolling out new products.

Wendel turned to the company's young ATV product manager, Matt Parks. Parks had quickly worked his way up the management ranks after joining Polaris as a district sales manager in 1987 and had impressed Wendel with his analytical skills. Now Wendel gave Parks a new responsibility: figuring out which new markets Polaris should enter next. As Parks would later recall, he attacked his new assignment using what might best be described as a shotgun approach.

Starting in early 1993, I was told to take a look at all these different markets: go-karts, golf carts, lawn and garden, chain saws, or whatever. I would find out about the industry and who the players were, how big it was, whether it was being well served, its new trends, and whatnot, and I'd present these findings to Hall.[3]

Named general manager of new products, Parks was inundated with solicitations from would-be

In 1998 Polaris introduced its fourth major product—Victory Motorcycles.

inventors and business partners. "I was sent every hula hoop and every Rube Goldberg device from every quack in the country," he said.[4]

But only one of the new markets Parks studied seemed to hold immediate promise: motorcycles.

For three months, ending in August 1993, Parks, with assistance from Bob Nygaard, Snow-

mobile division general manager, compiled as much information as he could on the motorcycle market. The two men hired outside consultants, collected sales numbers and technical specifications from motorcycle industry sources, and surveyed current Polaris vehicle owners to gauge their interest in motorcycles.

"The result of the study was, believe it or not, that yes, there was a tremendous opportunity in the motorcycle market," Parks said. Despite some misgivings ("I didn't really get too excited there," the normally gung ho Chuck Baxter confessed), company officers gave Parks permission to pursue the idea further. Parks gave the project a code name: Victory.[5]

Smells Like . . . Victory

Over the next three years, Parks's Victory engineering team, led by motorcycle industry veteran Geoff Burgess, turned the idea into chrome-plated reality. Team members tested other companies' bikes in the Arizona desert and tore them apart to see what they were made of. Some engineers worked on the motorcycle's overall design while others concentrated on producing, in house, an entirely new, big-bore, V-twin engine. In 1995 they cobbled together "Francis the Mule," the first of many prototypes. And in November 1996, they put engine and chassis together for the Victory's first test ride. Eighteen people gathered at Osceola's municipal airport to see and hear the new machine make its maiden runs up and down the airstrip. The Victory performed admirably, topping 100 miles an hour on several occasions.

Three months later, Polaris confirmed what had become an open secret: It was leaping into the motorcycle business. Polaris provided no details about specifications or price, but it did announce that the Victory would be a made-in-the-U.S.A. heavyweight cruiser that would compete head-to-head with Japanese manufacturers such as Honda, Kawasaki, Yamaha, and Suzuki. "We regard the Japanese as our primary competitors," Hall Wendel explained. "We met these guys in snowmobiles and ATVs, and we beat their asses off."[6]

At the same time, the company went to great lengths to appear downright submissive in the

Even before its unveiling, dealers, consumers, and the trade press were keyed up for the Victory V92C, which, in its debut year, became *Cycle World's* "cruiser of the year."

shadow of the cruiser market's dominant leader, Harley-Davidson. "We're not looking to be a real big player in the market," Ken Larson insisted. "We realize that Harley-Davidson has a tremendous amount of charisma. It will take a long time for this to be a major part of our business."[7]

Chuck Crone, plant manager at Spirit Lake, thought it would be a nice touch to assemble the first Victory motorcycle on July 4. The target date to build the first vehicle was only a few days after that, so the task didn't seem too difficult—except most of the workers had other plans for the holiday. Still, Crone had 12 volunteers who worked through the morning and into the afternoon to ensure that Victory would triumph on Independence Day. Hall Wendel rode the first Victory V92C out of the assembly plant in Spirit Lake on July 4, 1998. On that day, Polaris became the first American company to enter the motorcycle market in 60 years.

By that time, Polaris's new V-twin cruiser was already receiving accolades for combining the styling and power of a traditional cruiser with the superior handling of a sport bike. *Cycle World*, North America's largest motorcycle magazine, had named it "cruiser of the year" before it even hit the streets. "When a custom-styled machine can successfully blend stability and agility with adequate cornering capability like Victory has achieved with its V92C, I get a renewed sense of patriotic pride," *Cycle World*'s road-test editor wrote. Matt Parks proclaimed Victory the "first significant motorcycle widely distributed by a new American motorcycle manufacturer in 60 years."[8]

And all of a sudden, Wall Street couldn't help but notice.

The company's share price, which had been languishing the month before, bounced to near-record highs during the first few weeks after production began on the Victory. Industry analysts were impressed. "I think it's a worthwhile undertaking," one Chicago-based analyst said of the Victory project. "[The motorcycle market is] bigger than any other market that Polaris currently operates in. It's possible that in 10 years, motorcycles will account for the biggest percentage of Polaris revenues."

By introducing a new product that generated substantial and positive news coverage, Polaris had finally succeeded in raising its profile among

Hall Wendel (left) and Al Unser Jr., a two-time Indy 500 winner, astride the new Victory V92 cruiser at the motorcycle's coming-out party at Planet Hollywood on June 26, 1997. Unser Jr. had been riding Polaris products since he was a child, and as an avid motorcycle rider, he was happy to help Polaris kick off the Victory launch.

investors. But company executives still were not satisfied with the stock's performance. Clearly, product innovation was not, on its own, going to get the job done. If the company wanted to raise its profile even higher, it would need some fresh new direction from the top.

The New Guy

On July 15, 1998, less than two weeks after the first Victory rolled off the production line in Spirit Lake, Polaris witnessed its first major changing of the guard in nearly a decade. At age 37, Thomas C. Tiller, a former executive at General Electric, took over as Polaris's president and chief operating officer, succeeding the retiring Ken Larson. Larson had wanted to retire a year earlier, but Hall Wendel had convinced him to stay on until "we both agreed we had found the right person to succeed him," Wendel said. Tom Tiller, Wendel declared, was the right person.

"Hall was so excited about having found Tom," said David Mona, chairman of the Minneapolis office for Weber Shandwick, a public relations firm. Mona had been working with Polaris since 1984 and had done wonders in helping Polaris move its positive image into the public's eye. "Hall was very careful that he find somebody who would be accepted but who wasn't a clone, who had separate skill sets, and I think he chose wisely," Mona said. "Tom came in, and just as soon as he met people, they saw. He's not only eloquent, he's real. He's a person of substance but also the kind of guy you wouldn't mind going on a trip with."[9]

Tiller had the right résumé—degrees from M.I.T., Harvard, and the University of Vermont, and 15 years at General Electric. But he also had something that many other candidates for the position lacked—an affinity for the kinds of products Polaris made. "Tom grew up in Vermont and had his own motorcycle by the time he was 10," Wendel said. "He's a snowmobile and watercraft enthusiast. We couldn't be more excited to have him joining us."[10]

Tiller seemed just as thrilled as Wendel. "This is as exciting an opportunity as someone in consumer marketing can find," he told the *Minneapolis Star-Tribune*.[11]

Indeed, 15 minutes into his first conversation with Hall Wendel, Tiller had decided that he would probably take the job with Polaris. "You get a sense of people," he said, "whether somebody is a person you can trust, whether they're smart, whether they're a straight shooter, and I just very quickly got a positive impression that Hall would be a great person to work with and that Polaris would be a wonderful place to work."[12]

Tiller's polished communication skills and undeniable charisma only added to his long list of pluses. "Tom helps me do my job," said Richard Edwards, director of investor relations. "He doesn't mind going out and talking to investors, and he's very passionate about our business and our products."[13]

Tiller's stint as president and COO was actually something of an apprenticeship. In May 1999, 10 months after joining Polaris, Tiller replaced Hall Wendel as the company's CEO. Wendel stayed on as chairman of the board.

Tom Tiller became Polaris's new president and chief operating officer in 1998 and CEO in 1999. Tiller's sharp business sense and fondness for Polaris products made him a perfect leader for the company as it rode into the new millennium.

Changes for the Better

Tiller built a reputation for being down-to-earth, the kind of boss who knew the employees on a first-name basis and who blurred the inherent caste line between management and rank-and-file employees. As his assistant, Janet Klis, pointed out, "He treats everybody in the same way. There's no 'upper echelon' attitude here."[14] On a day when he was making a presentation to employees at the Roseau plant, for example, he rolled up his sleeves and joined the assembly line.

On his first day at Polaris, Tiller effectively put an end to the traditional suit-and-tie dress code by coming to work without a tie, and he didn't hesitate to make other changes as well. He made it clear from the beginning that he had big plans for Polaris. Before agreeing to take the position, he had spent six months reading everything he could get his hands on about the company and had visited with dealers and former employees to get their impressions. Thus when he arrived at work that first day, he already had a clear understanding of Polaris's strengths and weaknesses.

I saw Polaris as kind of an archery target with the product at the bull's eye because Polaris is really good at product. The next ring out is what produces the product, the engineering and manufacturing groups. Those were pretty strong. But the further you got from the product, the weaker the company's components. There was essentially no human resources function, for example, no head of purchasing. The core was strong; Polaris was a good company. But I thought we could turn it into a great company.[15]

Tiller began hiring new management talent—men and women who could take Polaris to the next stage in its evolution.

"Polaris had outgrown its systems," said John Corness, whom Tiller recruited from GE to head up Polaris's human resources functions. "When a company grows as fast as Polaris had, you outgrow a lot of the systems."[16]

"We had challenged ourselves to operate within the parameters we had," explained CFO Mike Malone. "That was our culture—to figure out a way to make it work."[17]

Polaris had been able to make do with the resources it had, but they restricted the company from moving to the next level of growth. Corness began what he called the "long, slow process" of building Polaris's human resources functions.

One of the first things we had to do was identify what we had because we didn't know what we had. There were no performance reviews. We had some org[anization] charts, but we didn't know who the people in the boxes were. We didn't know how many engineers we had with engineering degrees. We didn't know how many marketing people we had who had the capability to do market analysis.[18]

During 1999, his first year with Polaris, Corness conducted a comprehensive performance review of all the employees "so we knew who the good ones were, the superstars, and the ones we had to work on." He also raised the bar for new hires. "It takes a different skill set to run an accounting function for a $1.5 billion company versus a $3 billion company," he explained. "It's more complex, and we planned on being a $3 billion company. So we started to look at people who could operate in a $3 billion environment, and that's the screen we put on the new hires."[19]

Polaris was able to recruit from among the country's top talent. Its reputation as a fun, family-like place to work and its profit sharing plan made it particularly appealing, but Polaris also boosted salaries to make them more competitive, and senior managers were given free use of Polaris's products. In addition, almost all employees were shareholders through an employee stock ownership plan, or ESOP. "All the employees own Polaris stock," Corness said, "and not just a couple of shares either."[20]

One of Tiller's key hires was Ken Sobaski, who came on board in September 2001 as vice president of marketing and business development. Previously, Sobaski had been president of ConAgra's Grocery Brands division, where he implemented an aggressive growth strategy by focusing on brand revitalization, new products, and cost. Sobaski's goal at Polaris would be similar; Tiller wanted him to help Polaris build a dominant brand with industry-leading quality and service. Sobaski would also lead the company's growth initiatives.

In Tiller's opinion, the company had historically "taken kind of a Minnesota view: deliver the numbers, and the stock price will take care of itself." But with shares trading at a relatively modest ratio of 13 times earnings, he believed the company had to "do a better job of marketing . . . to the financial community."[21]

One of the things I did early on was get out on the road and meet with investors and explain who Polaris was and what we were trying to do. I thought it was very important to establish credibility early with the investment community. I had not done anything with Wall Street, and there was nobody here who really had, so we were feeling our way to a large extent. Also, this was just as the dot-com insanity was starting, so to say that the initial reception was a little cool would be a significant understatement. Nevertheless, we were knocking on a lot of doors.[22]

Tiller also stressed that Polaris needed to deliver on the financial commitment it made to the public. He observed that the company had missed its budget too often. "And there was always a good reason," he said. "Maybe it didn't snow. Or interest rates were wrong. Or we had a problem with a supplier. These are legitimate reasons, but the fact was, we missed the budget."[23]

That changed once Tiller came on board, and four years later he was able to declare with pride: "Investors understand that we're a company that delivers."[24]

Product innovation, as demonstrated by the Victory introduction, was another way to build awareness among investors, but not the only way. Tiller announced that the company was launching a series of "growth initiatives" that would guide Polaris "as we look to become a $2 billion company."[25]

Pure Polaris

Pure Polaris parts, garments, and accessories became a big part of "The Way Out" campaign. Pure Polaris, the company announced, took "the riding experience to the next level."

Although Tom Tiller insisted that he "did not want to turn this place into GE," he was determined to introduce to Polaris some of the business practices that made his former employer one of the most successful and admired companies in the world. Among the first concepts he transplanted to Polaris was known at GE as a service initiative, "the idea that rather than just going after trying to capture new customers, you look at your current installed base of customers and figure out how you can serve them better." Tiller wanted to apply the service initiative to a largely ignored segment of the company's business: parts, garments, and accessories (PG&A). And, Tiller said, the company to emulate in this regard was Harley-Davidson.[26]

To reflect its new service initiative, Polaris created an operating division called Pure Polaris to develop, market, and distribute Polaris's PG&A and to provide retail financial services, retail credit, and extended service contracts.

Pure Polaris got off to a roaring start, introducing 2,200 PG&A products in its first three years. The products were designed to complete the owners' riding experience and give them new ways to show off their pride as Polaris owners.

"Tom [Tiller] untied the one hand that was always tied behind my back, and we actually started investing in the PG&A business," said Bennett Morgan, then general manager for Pure Polaris. "Our traditional sales force has to take care of the snowmobiles, ATVs, and watercraft, and they generally have to cover 60 or 70 dealers. There's no time to talk about the 40,000 products we have in PG&A. Now we have our own sales force focused on servicing the dealer and the customer."[27]

By 2001 PG&A represented 14 percent of the company's total sales and had become Polaris's highest-margin business and the third-largest source of revenue, behind ATVs (56 percent) and snowmobiles (25 percent).

Pure Polaris also unveiled an e-commerce Web site at Pure Polaris.com to give customers the added convenience of ordering Polaris products on-line. The site included links to the Web sites of nearly 1,000 Polaris dealers and provided a platform from which the company could launch a new customization program. Under the Snow Check Select™ program, customers designed their own "dream machines" on-line, choosing everything from color and track and engine size to suspension options such as reverse or electric start—and ordered them for fall delivery through dealerships. Customers saved money, and dealers ended the season with less inventory because Polaris was able to build to customers' orders.

Dealers remained an integral part of the Snow Check Select™ program despite the new emphasis on e-commerce. "While we offer customization over the Internet, we opted against direct sales," Tiller said. "We wanted to use the Internet as a tool to strengthen the distribution network, not replace it."[28]

In 1999, through a partnership with Transamerica Corporation and later with Household, Pure Polaris introduced retail financial services at the consumer level, making it easier for consumers to purchase Polaris products. The company also formed a partnership with a warranty services company to offer extended service contracts and began offering consumer leasing.

The Polaris Starcard, a credit card that consumers could apply for at a Polaris dealership, offered consumers credit on anything sold in the dealership. "It's a revolving credit program that the dealer can provide to the consumer and get turnaround on approvals within five minutes of filling out a credit application," explained Scott Swenson, who succeeded Morgan as general manager of Pure Polaris.[29] The challenge, as Swenson saw it, was to convince more dealers to use Polaris's financial program over others'. "It's quick. It's simple," Swenson said. "There's a nice return for the dealer, and customers will be happy because they get approval quickly and can walk out of the store with their purchase."[30]

Creating Partnerships

Tiller's list of growth initiatives also included a new effort to forge alliances and partnerships that linked the Polaris name to other successful brands whose customers matched Polaris's core demographics: hardworking middle-class consumers. Polaris formed a partnership with the gun maker Remington and introduced a limited quantity of Sportsman 500 Remington® Special Edition ATVs, complete with camouflage patterning, a front rack extender, and tubular bumpers designed especially to appeal to hunters.[31] In a partnership with Ducks Unlimited®, Polaris raised more than $3 million to help restore wildlife habitat and in turn received increased visibility among the organization's 700,000 members with the donation of Ducks Unlimited® Special Edition ATVs. Polaris also formed marketing alliances with Dodge®, Bass Pro Shops®, Mossy Oak® (which sells one of the most popular lines of camouflage in the world), DeWalt® High Performance Tools, and Cabela's, a sports outfitter. A strategic alliance with machinery maker ASV Inc. gave Polaris the right to market and sell an ASV-built all-surface loader under the Polaris name (part of the Polaris Professional Series).[32]

Mossy Oak® Break-Up™ brand camo helps this Sportsman 500 blend into its surroundings, making it perfect for hunters.

Partnerships with professional sports organizations also presented ample opportunity to get the Polaris name in front of outdoors-minded people. NASCAR racer Kyle Petty became spokesperson for Victory, and Richard Petty, known as "the king" to NASCAR fans, became spokesperson for Polaris ATVs, which also sponsored Ward Burton's Number 22 car for the 2000 and 2001 Winston Cup and Busch Grand National Seasons. Polaris began shipping a Richard Petty Special Edition ATV in March 2002.

According to Petty, riding on a Polaris machine is "like riding a Rolls Royce instead of a go-kart. . . . I've got 600 acres behind my house," he said, "and 15 miles of trails. Me and the grandkids ride, and that's my escape. I get on the ATV, and I've got no telephone. Nobody knows where I am. It's the same with the snowmobile. We got a place in Wyoming where we ride, and it's just pure pleasure."[33]

In addition, Polaris sponsored the NFL, the NHL, and college hockey, as well as professional teams like the Minnesota Vikings football team and the Minnesota Wild hockey team.

Darcy Betlach, manager of corporate events and partnerships, couldn't hide her enthusiasm when it came to Polaris's bright future. "You'd better get a pair of sunglasses," she said, "because Polaris is going to be glaring. We're an asset to any company. We have a great story. We have a fantastic product. And we're not just a seasonal partner; we can fill a lifestyle need for these companies every season."[34]

The Way Out

Tom Tiller was insistent that Polaris build on its good name and turn itself into a brand that fostered allegiance across all product lines: snowmobiles, ATVs, PWCs, and motorcycles. As far as he was concerned, when it came to branding, Harley-Davidson was the gold standard. "For 46 years we've sold our products under the idea of selling a better mousetrap," he said, "but now we're really changing the basic proposition of selling products to the customer as an opportunity to get away from the stresses of everyday life."[35]

Polaris strengthened its brand by sponsoring the Number 75 Remington Arms/Polaris ATV Ford Taurus, piloted by Rick Mast (right). Polaris also participated in a variety of NASCAR-sponsored charitable fundraisers, thanks in large part to the efforts of Ed Skomoroh (left).

In early 2000, Polaris launched a new marketing campaign under the theme "The Way Out." Polaris's advertising agency, Martin/Williams, of Minneapolis, had developed the campaign after a survey found half of the 1,600 respondents felt "stressed out." With its new "The Way Out" message, Polaris was "shifting all its consumer communications to emphasize the escapist experience rather than 'mechanicspeak' about horsepower, suspension, and transmissions."[36] Tiller called the campaign "a long-term marketing change with the goal of building Polaris into a dominant worldwide brand."[37]

Polaris decided to get a jump on its new marketing campaign by turning to the past.

In the spring of 1999, Edgar Hetteen approached Ed Skomoroh about planning another snowmobile expedition across Alaska to coincide with the 40th anniversary of his Alaskan adventure in 1960, the one that had helped establish snowmobiling as a viable sport. "Edgar had been one of my first bosses at Arctic Cat, and over the years he kept talking about wanting to retrace his trip across Alaska," said Skomoroh.[38]

Skomoroh's mission at that time was to launch "The Way Out" campaign, so the timing for another Alaskan trip couldn't have been better. "All I needed to do was convince Tom Tiller that this is what we needed to do to launch the campaign," said Skomoroh.[39]

Tiller agreed so long as the expedition snagged the attention of the press and Wall Street.

"At first, Tom was not convinced that he had time to make the trip with us," said Skomoroh, "but a few days later he agreed. Now I had what I needed: Edgar, the original Alaskan adventurer and Polaris cofounder, and Tom, the new, young president. I knew I could launch an exciting new theme that would catch the interest of the financial world and consumers—and it did."[40]

David Johnson had not accompanied Hetteen on the first trip, but Tiller thought Johnson should join the 40th-anniversary journey. Johnson's son Mitchell, who was also Edgar Hetteen's nephew, had lots of experience with winter travel and camping out in the great outdoors. He joined the caravan as "wagon master" after planning the trip's itinerary and arranging all the gear and equipment.[41]

"Planning and going on that trip was probably one of my greatest joys," said Mitchell Johnson.

"I was 11 years old when Edgar made the first trip, and I remember that when they headed out, it was like they were going to the end of the world."[42]

In March 2000, Edgar Hetteen, Tom Tiller, David Johnson, Ed Skomoroh, Mitchell Johnson, Chuck Baxter, and four others set out on the "Breaking Trail" journey, a 900-mile snowmobile trek across Alaska. Mitchell Johnson even recruited Joey Turner, the nephew of Edgar's original guide, Alex Aloysius, to lead them across the same portage from the Kuskokwim River to the Yukon River in honor of both of their uncles.

Edgar Hetteen (center) greets his old friends Rudy Billberg (left) and Bessie Billberg (right) at the beginning of the Breaking Trail 40th-anniversary journey across Alaska.

The main goal of the 2000 trip was to launch "The Way Out" campaign to the world, especially the financial world. "We wanted to let them know that now Polaris was not just a snowmobile company but a world-famous recreational manufacturer," said Skomoroh. "We wanted to let them know that 'The Way Out' experience with Polaris, the escape from it all, encompasses many products and all ages."[43]

Hetteen, at age 79, played his role as the "Henry Ford of the snowmobile industry" for all it was worth. "At my age, the window of opportunity for this kind of adventure is closing quickly," he said. "More than anything, I want to prove to myself that I can still do it."[44]

And do it he did. Hetteen, the Johnsons, and their entourage, armed with satellite phones and a global positioning system, successfully completed the journey while providing twice-daily updates to a special Web site that tracked their progress.

During stopovers, the adventurers entered virtual chat rooms on the Internet to discuss the trip with interested parties. "My father wasn't coached," said Mitchell Johnson, "but what he was doing back in 1956 in terms of his vision for the snowmobile fits today our brand theme for the company. People would ask him why he built the first snowmobile, and it was interesting how he'd say, 'Well, we wanted a way to get out and enjoy winter and get away from our everyday lives.'"[45]

"It was a wonderful trip," said David Johnson. "We were raising money for the ALS [Amyotrophic Lateral Sclerosis] Association because one of our engineers has Lou Gehrig's disease. We were also promoting safety as much as we could. We stopped at schools along the way and visited with the Indian and Eskimo kids, and we'd always make sure they saw us with our helmets, and we'd tell them they should always wear a helmet when they're riding. Then Polaris sent some helmets to the schools to get them acquainted with safety products."[46]

"That was kind of my last hurrah," said Ed Skomoroh, who retired in June 2000 after 18 years with Polaris. "It was a great way to go into retirement: launch this campaign, ride with the Henry Ford of snowmobiles, and fade into the sunset."[47] Two years after his retirement, Skomoroh looked back fondly on his time with Polaris. "I ate, lived,

The Breaking Trail group prepares to embark on the 900-mile snowmobile journey across Alaska to introduce "The Way Out" campaign.

and worked Polaris," he said. "But it was the most exciting career of my life, and I even got paid for it."[48]

Once the Alaska adventure was complete, Polaris revved up its new branding campaign with "an aggressive 2000 advertising schedule" featuring print ads and television spots. While the campaign was designed to incorporate all of the company's major products, it concentrated first on snowmobiles. Humorous advertising copy reinforced the escapist impulses uncovered by consumer surveys.[49]

Polaris also jazzed up its communication with customers by embellishing its quarterly magazine. The magazine was first published in 1985 as *Spirit Magazine* and was mainly black and white. The name was changed to *Pro Spirit*, then *Polaris Pro*, and finally *Escape*, to better reflect "The Way Out" marketing campaign. By 2001, the magazine had evolved into a glossy, full-color format and was sent out to some 500,000 registered Polaris owners. But *Escape* did more than merely introduce customers to upcoming products. It also shared information about the best riding spots in North America and was sprinkled with editorials from enthusiasts who wrote in to tell Polaris readers about their "Way Out" experience.

As Polaris built its brand with the help of its new "The Way Out" campaign, it simultaneously worked to extend the brand to markets it had previously spent little time courting, especially the youth market. The company introduced a new youth model two-thirds-scale Indy XCR 120 snowmobile that brought "the legendary Polaris experience to a whole new demographic market."[50] In addition, it licensed a new die-cast Polaris ATV toy to appeal to toy collectors and a new video game called "Polaris SnoCross" for Nintendo and Sony PlayStation. The rationale behind a video game for teens and young adults was simple. Tiller said the game was "part of our overall effort to add exposure to the Polaris brand."[51] Such licensing agreements also produced income that wasn't dependent on vehicle sales trends.

Higher Expectations

Tiller also raised the standards by which Polaris benchmarked success. Rather than trying to outdo Arctic Cat, for example, he raised the competitive bar. "Arctic Cat is our crosstown rival," he said. "They're 60 miles away, and we thought if we could outdo Arctic Cat, we'd had a pretty good year. But the world is a much bigger place than just northern Minnesota."[52]

Backing up the company's new "higher standards" philosophy was a new system for tracking its success—or lack of it. According to Marlys Knutson, the system was based on what came to be known as Tiller points.

On a biweekly basis, we track every story that appears about Polaris. Tom established criteria for where he thought Polaris needed to appear from an importance standpoint, be it the Wall Street Journal, *be it* MSNBC, *be it* USA Today. *We had three different tiers, and each level had different points assigned to it: the financial press and large-city-based press, the medium-size-city press, and then the press for the Roseaus, the Osceolas—the small cities. Then on top of that, if the press mentioned "The Way Out," if they included a quote from Tom Tiller, or mentioned our Web site, additional points would be added. We started out with this being a corporate initiative and eventually started using it to track all of our divisional PR.*[53]

Each of Polaris's product divisions experienced ups and downs before Tiller kicked off the company's growth initiatives, but all of the divisions emerged from the company's new strategy stronger than ever.

Polaris touted the Indy XCR 800 as "the fastest 800 triple on snow thanks to its high-tech case reed engine design including triple pipes and variable exhaust."

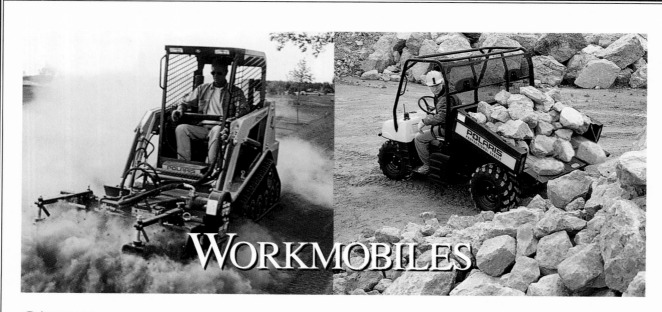

WORKMOBILES

SINCE THE POLARIS *RANGER*'S INTRODUC-tion in 1998, Polaris expanded the line to include 4x4 and 2x4 models. The company marketed the machine, in all its configurations, as "a ranch hand, trophy hauler, landscaper's dream machine, and a landowner's best friend."

After that, the company reached further into the commercial, off-road utility task vehicle (UTV) market and introduced the Polaris Professional Series, which turned standard-platform ATVs and Polaris *RANGER*s into durable Workmobiles™ for landscaping, cargo pulling, and other heavy-duty work.

"These are serious work vehicles," Polaris proclaimed, "loaded with features you won't find on other off-roaders." These features included rubber tracks designed to spread the machine's weight over a large surface, quick-attach tools, cargo boxes, dump-box lifts, flat beds, and more-powerful engines and "beefed-up" suspensions to increase towing capacity.

The Professional Series line included the ASL 300 (an all-surface loader), a full line of UTV vehicles, and the ATV Pro 4x4 and Light Utility Hauler 6x6. In 2002 Polaris Professional Series debuted the UTV 1500, which featured lowered suspension, easy bed access, and a powerful V-twin overhead air-cooled engine.[1] The company also introduced the PTV (personal task vehicle) 4x4 and 6x6, built to "provide the individual worker with access to the slickest, slimiest, and most treacherous job sites."[2]

The Workmobiles™ were so popular that in 2002 Polaris formed a new division, led by Ron Bills as general manager. One of Bills's first goals for the new division was to develop a quality distribution network, one that was appropriate for the Professional Series' specialized product. "We mean business," Bills said, "and we're just getting started."[3]

Polaris's Workmobiles™ are perfect for heavy-duty work.

The ATV Division

Polaris had brought more ATV product firsts to the industry than every other manufacturer combined, and the ATV division continued its record for innovation and quality. In 1997 the Sportsman 500 was rated the best ATV in the industry by several trade publications and continued to be the top seller in its category. In response to requests for a low-cost drive system with better durability, the Scrambler 400 and 500 models came out with Polaris's new Concentric Drive System. And the Sportsman 500's new High Output (H.O.) engine debuted as the most powerful four-stroke ATV engine in the industry.

In 1998, the company's ATV sales continued to climb, and Polaris, more than any of its competitors, increased its market share in the growing industry, thanks in part to its flexible manufacturing operations. All Polaris plants could handle multiple product lines and could switch quickly from one product to another as demand increased or declined.

The biggest ATV rollout in 1998 was an evolution of Polaris's Big Boss 6x6: the Polaris *RANGER,* a six-wheeled off-road utility vehicle with side-by-side seating. "[The Polaris *RANGER*] is a new product which will open the door for Polaris to the general purpose, off-road utility vehicle market," declared former ATV general manager Mitchell Johnson. "We are targeting farmers, hunters, and all types of construction activity, anything

requiring transportation on rough terrain."[54] Once again, Polaris was entering an established market—this time dominated by John Deere's six-wheeled Gator and Kawasaki's 4x4 Mule—but Polaris executives knew the company was up to the challenge.

All in all, the ATV division experienced phenomenal growth throughout the 1990s and into the new century. "We really redefined the ATV marketplace," said Bennett Morgan, who became general manager for the ATV division in 2001. "The dominant segment in the business is called a recreational utility segment, and there wasn't even a definition of that segment when we entered the market. We've brought a ton of innovation that other manufacturers are copying—automatic transmissions, big-bore 4x4s, independent rear suspension technology—and now we have to take our innovative spirit to the next level in ATVs."[55]

That's exactly what Polaris did. The Sportsman 700 Twin, unveiled in 2001, became the largest big-bore premium recreational utility ATV in the industry and was named "ATV of the Year" for 2002 by *ATV Magazine.* (Polaris also received the magazine's first Legacy Award for "revolutionizing the ATV industry and ATV riding.") The Sportsman 700 Twin was the most powerful and feature-rich ATV on the market and ran on Polaris's new four-stroke, liquid-cooled 700 Twin engine, the first ATV engine to be designed and built in the United States. No other 4x4 had an engine as large as the 700 Twin. In 2002 the ATV division rolled out a new sport and performance ATV called

After its launch in 1998, the Polaris *RANGER* line of utility ATVs quickly became one of the most exciting product lines in Polaris's growing stable.

Right: The Polaris Professional Series featured an all-surface loader built by machinery maker ASV Inc.

Below: The Trail Boss 330 was the world's best-selling automatic 2x4 ATV, just as the Sportsman 400 was the world's best-selling 4x4.

Right: The Polaris Professional Series featured an all-surface loader built by machinery maker ASV Inc.

Below: The Trail Boss 330 was the world's best-selling automatic 2x4 ATV, just as the Sportsman 400 was the world's best-selling 4x4.

the Predator. "[The sport and performance ATV] is a growing segment that caters to Gen X and older Gen Y riders who prefer lightning fast ATV racetracks and sand dunes over traditional trail riding," said Morgan.[56] The sleek, futuristic-looking Predator 500 had a new, high-performance engine and proprietary Polaris Rider Optimized (PRO) steering system, giving riders greater control and easier steering with a tighter turning radius. Polaris also offered a limited-edition Predator 500 with graphics designed by Troy Lee, renowned for his custom graphics and helmets.

Clearly, the Predator 500 was an industry favorite, for it racked up three "ATV of the Year" titles, from *ATV Sport,* Canada's *ATV Rider,* and *ATV Test Guide.* "With the Predator, Polaris blitzed the U.S. patent office with several engineering firsts," wrote *ATV Sport.* "The chassis itself includes

several impressive design features. But the interaction of the chassis, suspension and steering components—called the Polaris Rider Optimized (PRO) system—takes sport quad handling to another realm."[57] And *ATV Test Guide* wrote, "This ATV will increase, by another notch, the level of competition in this segment because of the innovations which make the smoothness and flexibility of its suspensions in a class by themselves."[58]

The Predator 90 Youth ATV, a smaller version of the Predator 500 designed for riders 12 and older, was also introduced in 2002. All of the Polaris youth models came with parent-adjustable speed controls and a whip flag plus a safety video and a helmet to encourage safe riding habits at a young age. Polaris also unveiled the Sportsman 600 Twin, a four-wheel-drive ATV with the traditional power of the Sportsman and independent rear suspension for a smooth ride.

Polaris muscled ahead of the competition with yet another product innovation in 2003. The Polaris All-Terrain Pickup (ATP), which debuted on NBC's *Today* show, created a new niche for ATV enthusiasts. A cross between an ATV and a pickup truck, the ATP was perfect for hunters, farmers, ranchers, campers, large estate owners, and outdoor recreation enthusiasts. The ATP had twice the storage capacity of typical ATVs and a rear cargo box that emptied like a dump truck. It also had a new "VersaTrac" drive system that operated in all-wheel or two-wheel drive and could be changed to "turf" mode for riding on lawns and other soft ground.

Roger Evans, senior research analyst at Craig-Hallum Capital, observed that Polaris was "bucking the trend" of slowing ATV sales by broadening its product lines.[59]

The Snowmobile Division

Though industry-wide retail sales of snowmobiles slowed due to low or late snowfall, Polaris continued to gain market share and to demonstrate its leadership position in the business it had pioneered.

For the 1998–99 season, Polaris overhauled its snowmobile line, unveiling 23 new models. The new snowmobiles racked up a number of awards. The Indy 600 RMK became *Snow West's* "Mountain Sled of the Year" for 1998; *Sno Goer Magazine's* "Sled of the Year" went to the 700 XCSP; *Snow West's* "Mountain Muscle Sled of the Year" went to the Indy 700 RMK; and *Snowmobile* magazine's "Best in Class" models were awarded to the 600 XC and 700 XC.

In 1999 *Snowmobile* magazine rated six Polaris models as "Best in Class." *Snow West* named the five RMK models "Mountain Sleds of the Year," the only time the award was given to an entire family of sleds. *American Snowmobiler* pinned awards on Polaris models in seven of eight classes.

Though industry-wide snowmobile sales were on a downward slide in 2000, Polaris was the only manufacturer to gain market share. For the 2000–01 season, the company introduced the next in a long list of innovations, the EDGE™ chassis, which was 10 pounds lighter than Polaris's previous chassis, had 150 fewer parts (thus reducing assembly costs and raising quality), and made for a smoother ride and easier handling.

Polaris continued to gain market share in 2001, and wholesale sales of snowmobiles climbed 22 percent over the year before. This success was due in part to the new Snow Check Select™ program, introduced the year before, which allowed riders to customize their snowmobile with factory-installed options. For 2001, Snow Check Select™ propelled a nearly 50 percent increase in preseason retail sales over the previous year. "Dealers and their customers loved [Snow Check Select™], and it's easy to see why," reported Hall Wendel and Tom Tiller. "The program allows buyers to specify the machine of their dreams, place the order in the spring, and take delivery of a factory-built customized sled in the fall."[60]

Polaris's outstanding new products also drove snowmobile sales. The 2001–02 lineup included the Indy Frontier, a full-size touring snowmobile with a quiet, fuel-efficient, four-stroke engine that reduced harmful emissions by more than 90 percent compared to the industry average and complied with proposed Environmental Protection Agency (EPA) and National Park Service requirements. Also new that year was the 440 Pro X Fan, designed for snocross riders. This extra-durable, nimble sled featured a 440-cylinder engine and was calibrated for competitive snocross riding.

Polaris's 2003 snowmobile lineup included a new 440 Pro X that was quicker and had better handling and better driver ergonomics than the previous year's model. The company also introduced two new Indy Frontier models and the Indy 800 Classic Touring, a limited-edition model with the new EDGE Touring™ chassis technology and more features for passenger comfort. The industry accolades persisted as well; the 2003 RMK Vertical Escape became *Snow West* magazine's "Sled of the Year."

The Personal Watercraft Division

Beginning in 1997, the personal watercraft industry suffered a significant decline in demand, due in large part to uncertainty about potential regulatory and legislative limits on PWC use.

The 2003 snowmobile lineup included the limited-edition Indy 800 Classic Touring model, featuring new EDGE Touring™ chassis technology and added features for passenger comfort.

Polaris responded by pulling back production and helping dealers clear out their inventory.

In the meantime, the company offered new features and models that lowered cost, improved quality, and made it a leader in environmentally friendly PWCs. The year 1998 signaled a new beginning in the personal watercraft industry with the introduction of Genesis, the first-ever four-passenger PWC. Moving with the trend toward cleaner, quieter watercraft, the Genesis featured Polaris's new sound-reduction technology, called Planet™, which made the Genesis 60 percent quieter than the industry average, and a direct-injection fuel-injection system that reduced emissions by 76 percent and used 35 percent less fuel than carbureted models.

Industry-wide sales continued to sink in 1999, but Polaris, once again, gained market share. That year Polaris introduced the Virage and Virage TX models, which incorporated the Planet™ sound-reducing technology.

When Ron Bills joined Polaris in 2000 as the personal watercraft division's general manager, he was already a veteran in the PWC industry and knew that Polaris needed to step up its efforts if it wanted to become a strong industry competitor. Though Polaris had done a good job of meeting environmental regulations, Bills thought the company's PWCs lagged somewhat in styling and performance. "Polaris did well in the early 1990s when it introduced the watercraft, but then there was little progression after that," he said.[61]

Bills set out to make some changes.

Though industry-wide PWC sales declined in 2000, Polaris saw a 9 percent increase in retail sales as it attracted new buyers through promotions and partnerships with designers, racers, and freestyle competitors.

Polaris continued to outperform the market in 2001 despite a weakened economy. Several bans on watercraft use were overturned, and some regulatory and legislative issues were eliminated. All of Polaris's new models featured Planet™ technology. The Virage i, like its predecessor, met EPA

The Polaris EX2100 Sport Boat, unveiled in 2003, is powered by a 240-horsepower Mercury Marine engine and is outfitted with a number of premium standard features, including a custom trailer, a stereo/cd player, a large ski locker, and plush upholstery.

2006 emission standards and featured a two-cylinder direct-injection engine "for the best fuel economy of any watercraft in the industry," said Bills. The Polaris Octane, a new stand-up, race-only model, appealed to racing enthusiasts.

Then in 2002 Polaris made a splash with an entirely new line of PWCs called MSX. With sport-bike-inspired styling, the MSXs incorporated luxury features and were designed with a proprietary hull for aggressive turning ability and smooth, dry, stable cruising for up to three passengers. Polaris entered the four-stroke engine watercraft segment with two revolutionary MSX models, the MSX 110 and MSX 150. Both had turbocharged, low-emission engines that offered a superior horsepower-to-weight ratio. As Bills observed, "There's been a huge evolutionary process in the engines driven by consumer demand and EPA requirements, and Polaris continues to be on the forefront of that technology. The direct-injection four-stroke engine

is going to be the engine of choice for the long-range future."[62]

The MSX 140 H.O., equally sleek in appearance, had a direct-injection two-stroke engine, one of the cleanest and technologically advanced engines available. "The new Polaris MSX is the benchmark for others to follow," declared Bills. "This boat has passion and soul in a total package—from futuristic design, superior handling, and versatile performance to the unmatched automotive-quality fit and finish."[63]

Polaris diversified even further in the marine industry with the Polaris EX2100 Sport Boat line, which debuted in the spring of 2003. Polaris designed the new boat and allied with Baja Marine, a division of Brunswick Corporation, to manufacture it. Baja had a reputation for incorporating modern technology into the boat-building process, according to Bills. In a separate partnership, Mercury Marine, also a division of

In 2003 Polaris debuted its MSX line of personal watercraft. (Below: MSX 140, inset: MSX 150.) The sleek, futuristic-looking MSX could carry up to three people and featured turbocharged, low-emission engines.

Brunswick, equipped the sport boats with Mercury's proven Jet Drive technology.

"The Polaris EX2100 is not your dad's runabout," said Bills. "The futuristic new look of the EX2100 stands out with a progressive design that further reinforces the 'New Polaris Watercraft' image: unparalleled styling, a premium fit and finish, and a futuristic appearance."[64]

The Victory Division

Polaris sold more than 1,000 Victory motorcycles during 1998, the debut year, and cruised into 1999 with a backlog of orders, selling more than 3,000 units for the year. Also in 1999 the company introduced the world's first SportCruiser, the Victory V92SC, which combined cruiser styling with industry-leading handling. As Polaris pointed out, "The aging sportbikers . . . wanted a fast-handler with more cushion, and the current cruiser owners wanted a comfy bike with more spunk."[65] That year the V92C, Victory's original model, won *Motorcycle Cruiser* magazine's "Cruiser of the Year" award, and in 2001 the V92SC was named "Sport Cruiser of the Year" by *Easy Riders.*

In 2000 Victory's retail sales accelerated 50 percent over 1999, and the company upped its number of Victory dealers from 275 to 300. That year's model lineup offered more than 200 engineering changes and design improvements (while decreasing cost by 10 percent), including a redesigned transmission and new clutch.

According to power sports industry veteran Mark Blackwell, who was appointed general manager of the Victory division in 2000, Victory suffered a sort of identity crisis for its first few years, but eventually it found its niche.

We were trying to find out who we were going to be in the marketplace. Harley was all about mystique, so one of our first ideas was, "With Victory, you get less mystique, more motorcycle." Then we refined that position. Victory motorcycles essentially have better handling than Harleys or the Japanese bikes, so now we're "Victory, The New American Motorcycle." Harley is kind of the old guys, and we're the new guys: a little less retro-looking bike,

a little more forward-looking bike in terms of the styling, and a little more forward technology.[66]

As engineer Gary Gray proudly declared, "We're open to new ideas. We bring out new technologies. Typically, motorcycles lag behind automotive industry technologies—in some cases 10 years. But we don't let tradition bind us."[67]

Indeed not. The first Victory bikes featured four valve heads, whereas most other V-twins had only two. In addition, all Victory bikes came equipped with fuel-injected engines; other manufacturers offered fuel injection only as an option.

Victory also began building up a lifestyle image. Not only were Victory motorcycles American-made; Victory owners could become part of an owners' group, a sort of club that involved camaraderie built around activities and rides. "People who enjoy motorcycles, particularly cruisers, like the independence and freedom of the open road," said Blackwell, "but they also like to hang out with other motorcyclists."[68]

Owners also received a quarterly newsletter, were offered 24-hour roadside assistance, and

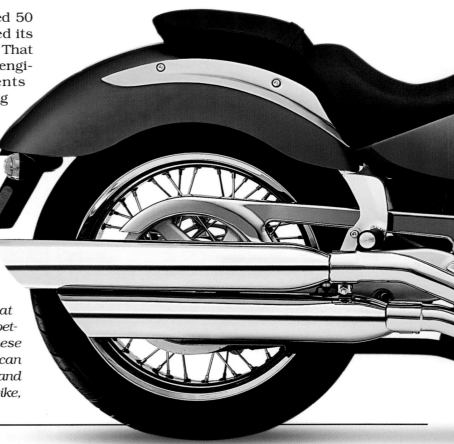

became members of the Victory Riders Association, which in its debut year sponsored 32 organized rides all over the country. "We've selected 16 regional

Renowned motorcycle designers Arlen and Cory Ness contributed to the completely new design of the Victory Vegas, part of the Victory 2003 lineup.

coordinators who are Victory customers who meet certain criteria," said Blackwell. "We send them a ride kit, and each of them will put on two rides that they organize through dealers."[69]

"The Victory Riders Association has been wildly successful," said Darcy Betlach, who conceived of the program while she was marketing manager for Victory. "The owners are almost infectious with excitement over the program."[70]

In addition, Victory began the Victory Custom Order program, much like the snowmobile division's Snow Check Select™ program, in which buyers could put down a deposit and custom design their motorcycles, choosing from more than 500 configurations. "It's a huge competitive advantage," said Blackwell. "[It] will change the way people think about how to buy a motorcycle."[71]

By 2001 Victory's profit margins had significantly improved, and though the division's $19 million in sales represented only 1 percent of Polaris's total, the company's leaders were confident that Victory would see rapid growth now that it had found its niche. As Mike Malone pointed out, "Victory is our best, biggest, long-term opportunity for growth."[72]

Victory's 2002 lineup featured the new Freedom™ V-Twin engine, which offered 25 percent more power and 10 percent better fuel economy. Unlike other major bike companies, which offered their new, more powerful engines in only one model, Polaris launched its new engine in its entire lineup. The company also expanded its customer base to include the fast-growing touring sector with the V92TC Touring Cruiser, offered in both standard and deluxe models.

Meanwhile, master custom bike builder Arlen Ness and his son Cory Ness became increasingly involved in providing input to the Polaris industrial design team and in developing the Arlen Ness Signature Series of Victory accessories. Arlen Ness was arguably the best-known and most-respected custom motorcycle builder in the world, and Cory Ness, with several well-known custom bikes under his belt, was on his way to becoming equally distinguished. The father and son team's custom bike and accessory business, which included a Victory dealership, tested new merchandising and sales approaches for Victory, and both Nesses made personal appearances on behalf of Victory at dealer meetings, press launches, and consumer events.

In the summer of 2002, Polaris unveiled a custom cruiser called the Victory Vegas. As the lead industrial designer for this groundbreaking motorcycle, Michael Song, with contributions from Arlen and Cory Ness, designed the overall appearance of the bike.

"We wanted to do something more than the typical teardrop tank," Song told *American Motorcyclist* magazine.[73]

"The centerpiece is the stretched tank," the magazine reported. "Arching gracefully over the top of the motor and lapping the front seat.... Elsewhere, stylish touches abound, like the unique spine running along the center of the bike, from the tip of the front fender, along the top of the fuel tank and down the rear fender.... This bike can be ridden all day, which is saying something when a motorcycle looks this good."[74]

Or, as Song told *Cycle World,* "The raised spine running tip-to-tail ties all the pieces together, allowing the fuel tank to serve as a focal point with the fenders growing out of it."[75]

The completely new design showed off, in the words of Gary Gray, lead engineer on the Vegas, "a lot of wheel and the most gorgeous set of body work I've ever seen on a motorcycle." The bike was built on a new chassis that was lower and longer than those of previous Victory motorcycles and included an updated version of the Freedom™ V-twin engine and oodles of cutting-edge technology. True to its image as The New American Motorcycle, the Vegas featured an LED taillight, "which is brand new to the automotive industry," said Gray. "We're one of the first motorcycle cruisers to have the LED."[76]

Jeff Whaley, a Victory dealer in Cumming, Georgia, near Atlanta, described the Vegas's design and styling this way: "It looks like it's going 100 miles an hour sitting still."[77]

"Victory's strength from the beginning always has been good handling and braking performance," reported *Cycle World.* "The Freedom engine added refinement and power to the package. Fuel-injection calibration just doesn't get much better than this. Power delivery is what you would expect of a 1507cc V-Twin.... Vibration levels are very low for a big Twin.... Shifting has been improved yet again."[78]

"Polaris's bikes get better and better," said Arlen Ness. "If you know anything about Polaris, everything they make, whether watercraft or snowmobiles or ATVs, it's the best in the industry. My son and I really enjoy working with them because they're up to doing some neat new things. It might take another company 10 years to do something that Polaris does in a year."[79]

For the future, Blackwell planned to incorporate even more forward looking styling and technology in Victory's design. Polaris partnered with Visteon, a spin-off company of Ford, which had been supplying Victory's computerized fuel-management and spark-ignition control, to build a concept bike that represented Victory's vision of its future. Victory's industrial design department, under Todd Dannenberg, designed the bike, and Visteon, which wanted to show its commitment to motorcycles and showcase its technology, built it.

Polaris displayed the concept bike, appropriately called "Vision," at auto and motorcycle shows around the country. Vision featured such futuristic amenities as thumbprint identification, keyless ignition, Internet access, a global positioning system, a voice-activated cell phone, and an intercom between rider and passenger.[80]

A Global Presence

While Polaris continued to shine in domestic markets, it also began to significantly grow its international presence. In 1997 Polaris's international sales increased 20 percent over the previous year, but in 1998 its international business still represented less than 6 percent of sales. With the goal of becoming a truly global company, Polaris stepped up its efforts to grow its international market share and hired Dick Pollick as vice president of international operations.

Pollick and his team focused on creating a strong international distributor network and established wholly owned subsidiaries in Australia, New Zealand, France, the United Kingdom, Norway, and Sweden. Their efforts quickly paid off; international sales grew 11 percent in 1999 and an amazing 22 percent in 2000.

The company also had a number of contracts with the U.S. government and U.S.-allied governments. After the September 11, 2001, terrorist attacks, the United States began using Polaris watercraft and snowmobiles for military training and homeland security. In addition, allied forces in search of the enemy in Afghanistan depended on Polaris's ATVs for transportation. "The military already used Polaris snowmobiles," said Greg Hedlund, international service representative. "Then they found out that we made ATVs and knew they'd be reliable and durable."[81]

Allied countries also used Polaris *RANGER*s for border patrols, and Polaris outfitted nearly 100 ATVs with military gear and shipped them overseas for military use. The Sportsman 700 Twin, for example, was ideal for climbing the narrow, rocky mountain trails of Afghanistan.[82] When the government began mandating safety training for the ATVs, Polaris experts, including Greg Hedlund, certified a number of soldiers as instructors so they could then train their peers."[83]

Just after the war on Iraq began in March 2003, Polaris contracted with the U.S. Army to build hundreds of uniquely equipped Sportsman ATVs. They were outfitted with infrared headlights, sport towing winches on the front and back, two gas tanks, machine gun mounts, and attachments for a stretcher. "The racks are twice the size of the normal ATV," Tiller explained. "So instead of carrying a deer or elk, you can carry four or five beefy soldiers if someone is shooting and you need to get them out of harm's way in a hurry. You can carry men, fuel, ammunition."[84]

Though the percentage of international sales by product line was similar to that of domestic sales (with ATVs accounting for 55 percent of international sales in 2002), Carmen Kwong, international product manger, pointed out that the uses for the products were "vastly different." ATVs, for example, target "primarily an agricultural or strictly on-road market abroad," Kwong explained. "The ATV was developed here in the United States for off-road use, but we've actually adapted it for on-road use in Europe."[85]

The durability of Polaris *RANGER*s makes them perfectly suited for use by the U.S. military and allied countries.

Dealing with the Best

Recognizing that dealers were integral to giving customers the ultimate experience, Polaris took its partnership with dealers to the next level. Tom Ruschhaupt, former vice president of sales and service, explained the importance of strengthening Polaris's dealer base and of retaining quality dealers. "Having an innovative product and a quality product will always be key to Polaris's growth," he explained. "But Polaris isn't necessarily in full control of customer loyalty. The dealer, the person who is in contact with the consumer, is key to creating customer loyalty, key to Polaris's growth."[86]

Ruschhaupt's team focused on strengthening dealers' performance by improving the Polaris-dealer relationship. For as Ruschhaupt pointed out, "The dealers have to be enthusiastic advocates of our products in order to sell them."[87]

Polaris further refined its dealer councils (created in 1988 under Ken Larson's direction) so that dealers could help decide when and how often new products should be introduced. Jeff Whaley joined the Victory dealer council in 2001 and was impressed with how Polaris's management listened to what the dealers had to say: "Mark Blackwell and Tom Tiller will sit there and say, 'Okay, guys, tell us what color the grass is.' We tell them, and they actually listen."[88]

When dealers said they wanted more information, more training, and more ways to delight the customer, Polaris established a toll-free dealer hotline and opened University of Polaris training centers, where dealer associates received classroom and Web-based training. The company also developed electronic report cards as a way for dealers to share information on improving customer satisfaction and sent Polaris managers to spend time with dealers so they could better understand their perspective.

Polaris also stepped up its efforts to monitor retail sales and adjust production to demand so that dealers didn't get stuck with excess inventory. In 2000 Polaris tested a new ATV replenishment initiative with select dealers. Instead of having to forecast their model mix and demand far in advance, ATV dealers received a replacement ATV each time a particular model was sold. The Snow

Below and opposite: The company's sport-model watercraft combined power with versatility.

Check Select™ and Victory Custom Order programs also helped control inventory.

In addition, Polaris's new Power Merchandising Program helped dealers redesign their showrooms with "The Way Out" custom fixtures and displays to stimulate sales. Dealers could benefit from wholesale financing, receive capital assistance grants, and participate in performance-based incentives. The company also invested in grassroots advertising and marketing, processed claims more quickly, and reorganized the sales force so that dealers had easier access to their district sales manager—all to help dealers build their business and boost the Polaris brand.

Polaris even opened a 20,000-square-foot service-oriented prototype superstore in Atlanta, Georgia, called Polaris America of Atlanta, where, "if it's not Polaris, we don't sell it," said Ben Blackmon, the store's vice president and general manager. "This store is part of what we feel Polaris wants the dealerships to look like and be like

in the future," he said. "The people at Polaris pay close attention to us. They listen to our needs. They support us, and with that kind of support, our numbers have done nothing but climb."[89] In only 16 months after its grand opening, Polaris America of Atlanta had gained 22 percent of the area's market share.

Information technology played a vital role in assisting dealers with their business. Bill Fisher, chief information officer, pointed out that dealers ordered 92 percent of their inventory electronically, which meant the company's information technology capabilities had to be cutting edge. "Our electronic ordering gives dealers visibility to current inventory, so they know what's available when they order it," Fisher said. "We've also put in place a feature that lets dealers track their orders through UPS, which helps them serve the customer better. When a customer calls and asks where a part is, the dealer can tell them where it is and when it will arrive."[90]

Market Driven

One of the hallmarks of Polaris's success had always been the quality of its engineering and its spirit of innovation. Polaris retained those qualities but also shifted toward being more market driven, toward giving consumers more of what they wanted.

As Judy Kulsrud, sales operations manager, explained, "We're not only focusing on the dealer; we're also focusing on the consumer. In the past, we didn't have a lot of tools that we gave to dealers to get them to understand the consumer and what the consumers are doing, but now we're driving more focus on the consumer from the dealer level through training."[91]

That focus on the consumer also meant staying on the cutting edge of not only engineering but also design and styling. "You shouldn't try to rationalize to anybody why they need a snowmobile or personal watercraft or ATV," said Todd Dannenberg, manager of industrial design. "Instead, you want to make them fall in love with it." And, Dannenberg explained, Polaris could make consumers fall in love with Polaris products by studying what will appeal to them four or more years before a product's release and

by targeting the designs to specific audiences. "There's no more designing by consensus," he said. "We want to create designs that polarize people's opinions because that's what creates the emotional hook."[92]

Beginning around 2002–03, Polaris's products began featuring more "edgy" designs than in the past. "You'll see a lot of crisp edges and a lot of geometric forms," said Dannenberg. "That's one trend."[93]

As it did with dealers, information technology played a vital role in enhancing customers' experience. PolarisIndustries.com, for example, gave consumers valuable information about Polaris products. They could make purchases on the Web or find a nearby Polaris dealer. The site also featured a parts catalog "so that people can find the part they need and actually bring the diagram into the dealer," explained Bill Fisher. In addition, the Web site provided detailed product information, product comparisons, and service manuals. Customers could enter special chat rooms to exchange information or riding stories and could access trail maps, event schedules, and riding and safety tips. The site even provided technical tips. If, for example, a customer wanted to install a plow on his snowmobile and had lost the instructions, he could type in the question and bring up the information.

Customers could also join special programs such as the Preferred Registered Owners Family. These informed, responsible riders were offered exclusive merchandise, competitive insurance rates for their Polaris vehicles, and special group rides and package tours. At the same time, the members provided Polaris with important feedback on their riding habits and product needs.

The Experience

Even while Polaris evolved into a $1.5 billion corporation, the company managed to retain the passion and spirit first instilled by founders Edgar Hetteen, Allan Hetteen, and David Johnson.

Speaking at a dealer convention in 1999, Ed Skomoroh coined a phrase that would become Polaris's slogan when he announced three commandments Polaris had to live by if it wanted to successfully deliver "The Way Out" experience

to customers: "Understand the riding experience. Live the riding experience. Work to make it better."

Tom Ruschhaupt reflected on why it was so important for employees to live the experience.

We were having a quarterly business review and were talking about how to improve the experience. Someone mentioned, "Well, we could put a compass on every snowmobile so we could advertise that you could never get lost on a Polaris snowmobile." One of the guys from Roseau who had been with Polaris for a long time and was an avid snowmobile rider looked up and, as sincere

Polaris customers who join the Preferred Registered Owners Family program are offered exclusive merchandise and special group rides and package tours.

as the day is long, said, "Well that will take all the fun out of it."[94]

To encourage employees to "live the experience," the company sponsored "Way Out" rides in which employees took field trips to ride the company's products. The lots at Polaris's various offices included parking sections for snowmobiles, ATVs, and motorcycles. And Polaris kept fleets of snowmobiles and ATVs that employees could take out on the weekends. Polaris headquarters in Medina, Minnesota (the company moved to the new building in January 2000), was located on a snowmobile trail so employees could ride to work. "So the whole experience is built into the building as well," said Scott Swenson.[95]

The Polaris Experience Center in Roseau, which opened in December 2001, featured product displays, enlarged photos, lifelike exhibits, and video presentations to guide visitors through Polaris's history. "The comments we've had since we opened have been unreal," said Lyle Grindy, coordinator of the Experience Center. "We're just really proud of it, not only for Polaris and its employees but also for the Roseau area."[96]

Industry-Leading Quality

In addition, Polaris began a new industry-leading quality initiative in 2000 as part of an overall effort to build a dominant brand. As Bruno Silikowski, director of supply chain quality, pointed out, "Solid product quality plus processes that support a dealer's ability to provide value to consumers are prerequisites to building a dominant brand. Our goal is to achieve industry-leading quality in our products and processes."[97]

The initiative, Silikowski explained to Polaris employees, "is very much in line with our 'The Way Out' campaign. To achieve industry-leading quality, we must begin by understanding what our consumers think is important and design it into our products and processes. By designing what our consumers value and by leveraging Polaris's innovation, we will be creating 'The Consumer Experience.'"[98]

To accomplish this huge task, Polaris conducted market research to find out what consumers thought was important. "We start with the consumer in mind," Silikowski said, "and drive that back through all of our processes. Instead of building it and they will come, it's more about building it with the consumer in mind—thinking about what they really care about. We used to build products more from technical innovation, and now we're becoming much more consumer focused, giving the consumer more of the value they're looking for in addition to our innovation."[99]

Based on the market research, the general managers and their teams for each product group worked together to define goals and create action plans. Polaris also launched improvement initiatives in each business area and continuously monitored progress and made corrections where necessary.[100]

The drive toward industry-leading quality became a part of Polaris's culture, Silikowski explained, a mindset that started at the top and was passed on to each and every employee. "We've communicated to employees a clear vision of what the changes are and what we want them to achieve," said Silikowski, "and we give them the skills to make those changes. Every single employee will receive the basic training that we have deployed, and from there, different levels of training and skills will be brought to each group."[101]

Polaris People

One of Polaris's best and most unique features is its culture, a culture in which people are recognized as the company's greatest asset. "We do surveys to keep our finger on the pulse of the organization," said LaRae Krahn, human resources manager for Roseau's engineering group. "We ask what makes working at Polaris so good, and over and over they say it's the people. Sure, the benefits are nice, the products are fun, but it's the people they work with who make the work rewarding."[102]

"The culture of this company is phenomenal," said Tiller. "It's a lot different from the business culture that I've always worked in. The loyalty of the people to the company and the company to the people is incredible."[103]

"Being number two isn't good enough for any of us," said Tim DeJong, director of materials, logistics, and manufacturing systems. "That attitude traces back to the culture of Roseau, and it permeates everything we do. It's a really unique environment to work in."[104]

THE ROSEAU FLOOD BRINGS OUT THE BEST

IN THE SUMMER OF 2002, HEAVY RAINS flooded the Roseau River, causing it to crest to more than 23 feet, seven feet above flood level. On June 11 the swollen river could be contained no longer, and a dike burst, threatening Roseau with cataclysmic devastation. In an astounding display of human compassion, determination, and unity, Polaris employees worked with residents of Roseau and northern Minnesota to save the town.

Local volunteers, city and county workers, and National Guard members worked late into the night, stacking sandbags to save the hospital, the high school, the Roseau County Sheriff's Office—and the Polaris plant, the largest employer in town. "Workers focused on saving the plant because of the significant economic impact it has on the area," reported the *Star Tribune.*[1]

Tom Tiller was among the Polaris volunteers who fought the flood on the front lines. He spent the morning, afternoon, and night of June 11 packing sandbags, pumping water, coordinating with emergency response people, and directing Polaris's fleet of ATVs, Workmobiles, and utility task vehicles, which were used to build and strengthen dikes, transport sandbags, and travel across muddy waters and roads where trucks and large equipment couldn't reach.

Tiller and other Polaris volunteers spent 20 minutes coming up with a game plan to save the Polaris plant, "and that probably made the difference," said Dean Hedlund, ATV development supervisor.[2]

"I was here all night with about 500 people building a barrier around the entire [Polaris] building," Tiller told the *Star Tribune.* "People worked all night flying up generators and 90,000 sandbags and pumps and all the other stuff we needed."[3]

Arctic Cat, Polaris's Minnesota rival, even paid the wages of two bus loads of people who came to help Polaris save its plant.

All the hard work and fortitude paid off. By the next day, the Polaris facility and its inven-

Polaris's people had always been deeply committed and loyal to Polaris, for as they saw it, Polaris was their company, and only more so because they were offered stock options.

"Each of us feels like we're an owner," said 38-year veteran Marlys Brandt a few months before her retirement in 2002. "I love Polaris. I love working here."[105]

And Polaris employees showed a willingness to go the extra mile to help the company—an outlook that attained some very tangible material benefits for Polaris. Sales per employee were nearly twice as high as the industry average.

"Nobody here is afraid to roll up their sleeves and get out there," said Duane Osell, a 36-year Polaris veteran who worked in project engineering and facilities engineering. "When the job has got to get done, it gets done."[106]

"It's unbelievable what our people can do," said Marlys Olsen, supervisor of brakes and struts. "People are real assets—they're everything. We've always continually improved the way we do things, and that's because we listen to the employees."[107]

Tiller expressed his amazement at Polaris employees' remarkable dedication. "There's an enormous pressure from the workers' peers to do well for the company, to not let the company down," he explained. "The people here have an unbelievable confidence in each other and in our ultimate ability to be successful at everything we do. It's that tremendous Midwest work ethic. We make mistory were "dry and intact," said Tiller, who made it clear that his main concern lay with Polaris's employees, their families, and their town of 2,700 people. Tiller kept the Roseau plant closed for the next few days so that employees could focus on saving their homes and helping their families and neighbors. Crews of Polaris employees with Polaris ATVs, Workmobiles, pumps, and generators went from house to house to remove water from basements and provide electricity for those battling the deluge.

Months later the town was still affected by the devastation. The downtown stores had set up shop elsewhere, and many of Roseau's homes and businesses had been severely damaged. Yet the town's residents felt blessed, for they lived in a community that had pulled together in their time of need. As Tiller said on the day after the dike broke, "If I wasn't so tired, I'd be crying right now. It's such a terrible human catastrophe, but through the whole ordeal I did not see a single person complaining. Everyone was working together in a way that just made me extremely proud, not just for the plant, but for the town."[4]

Tom Tiller, president and CEO, was among the Polaris people who volunteered to fight the Roseau flood on the front lines.

takes, but we know that if we stick together, we can figure out how to do just about everything."[108]

Such loyalty did not come by chance, for Polaris's leaders showed an uncommon appreciation for employees. That's one of the reasons Richard Edwards, director of investor relations, decided to join Polaris. "When I started looking around for new employment, I wanted a close-knit type of company, one that took care of employees and cared about them. Polaris fit right into that mold. The company is very considerate of the employees, treating them more like family than employees."[109]

Even those outside the company recognized Polaris's unique culture. "They run it like a family business," said Richard Petty. "Everybody works together, and I think that's why they're so success-

ful and why they've got such good products. They're so proud of their products. They just want to keep making them better."[110]

A Company in Good Hands

In 2001 Chuck Baxter retired, after 30 years of service, but as he pointed out, "I haven't fully retired. I call it semiretirement because it's hard to leave."[111] Baxter's ingenuity and innovative spirit had helped lead the company into new products, specifically the ATV, the personal watercraft, and the *RANGER*.

Secure in the knowledge that he was leaving the company in good hands, Hall Wendel stepped down as chairman of the board in May 2002, just after the annual shareholders meeting. (Bob Moe, Polaris's retired CFO, gave up his place on the board during the same meeting.) Tiller had proven to be an excellent leader, and the management team was primed and ready to face whatever challenges the future held. Gregory R. Palen became Polaris's new chairman of the board. A director since 1994, Palen was chairman and CEO of Spectro Alloys, an aluminum manufacturing company, and CEO of Palen/Kimball, a heating and air conditioning company.

Also that summer, Dick Pollick retired as director of international operations and was replaced by Mike Dougherty, who had spent the past two years in France growing Polaris's European sales and establishing its France and U.K. subsidiaries. In March 2003, Mary McConnell joined Polaris as vice president and general counsel.

The Polaris board of directors had evolved significantly and was now stronger than ever. In 1982, when the management partnership had scraped together the money to buy Polaris from Textron, the board comprised mainly people who had a significant emotional investment in the company. Even after Polaris became a publicly traded company in 1987, the board continued to function as though Polaris were a smaller, private company; the directors were friends and business associates who fulfilled their fiduciary responsibilities with very little debate. Not until Tiller came on board in 1998 did Polaris make a concerted effort to build a board made up of people from outside the company, seasoned professionals with diverse backgrounds in such areas as academia, business, financing, manufacturing, engineering, and law. That's when the board began playing a more active role. Not only were the nine directors involved in governing the company and doing so with honesty and integrity; they also reviewed and questioned the company's strategies and offered differing opinions, which resulted in well-rounded leadership for Polaris.

In 2002 Polaris's board comprised Gregory R. Palen as chairman of the board; Andris A. Baltins, an attorney with Kaplan, Strangis and Kaplan; George W. Buckley, chairman and CEO of Brunswick Corporation; William E. Fruhan Jr., professor of business administration at Harvard Business School; John R. Menard Jr., president

of Menard Inc.; R. M. (Mark) Schreck, president of RMS Engineering; J. Richard Stonesifer, president and CEO of GE Appliances; Thomas C. Tiller, Polaris's president and CEO; and Richard A. Zona, CEO of Zona Financial LLC.

Revved Up for the Future

Though many industries and corporations suffered in the post–September 11, 2001, recessionary economy, Polaris—thanks to strong leadership, innovative products and programs, world-class marketing, and dedicated employees, dealers, and partners—continued succeeding at full throttle.

Sales for 2001 rose 6 percent higher than the previous year's, reaching a record $1.5 billion. Net income increased 10 percent to $91.4 million, and earnings per share grew 11 percent to $3.88, marking the 20th consecutive year of earnings growth. A total yield of 48 percent to shareholders significantly outperformed the market. Since 1997, in fact, Polaris had outperformed the S&P 500 index, with a total return to investors of 173 percent, compared to 66 percent for the S&P 500.

Robert Evans, managing partner and senior research analyst with Minneapolis-based Craig Hallum Capital, was the first analyst to follow Polaris, beginning in 1995, and had nothing but praise for the company. "Despite a very difficult economic period, Polaris has not only met expectations but exceeded them," he said. "I think the misperception over the years has been that Polaris is a highly cyclical stock and that in a recession, the results would dip significantly. But in fact the company put up a record year for 2001."[112]

Evans wasn't the only industry watcher who realized how secure Polaris's stock was. As the *Wall Street Journal* reported in August 2002, "[W]hen hard times strike, sales could be expected to drop at Polaris Industries Inc. . . . But with the economy recovering only haltingly and the stock market suffering withering declines, Polaris is thriving."[113]

The article went on to highlight Polaris's impressive financial performance: "Overall, net income for the second quarter [of 2002] increased 16%, to a record $19.9 million—even as the Dow Jones Industrial Average was down about 12% at the end of June from a year earlier."[114]

Joe Hovorka, an analyst with Florida-based Raymond James, noted the consistency of Polaris's performance and attributed it to the company's leadership. "Polaris is probably one of the best managed companies within the recreational group," he said. "If you look at the kind of metrics and the kind of numbers this company has put out over the last several years, it's quite impressive. They have a return on equity that is greater than 40 percent. That's a number you'd be hard pressed to find many companies matching, and Polaris does that consistently while also producing consistent earnings growth. The company also has a lot of free cash flow, and they use that to buy back stock, which is also beneficial to the shareholders."[115]

"Polaris has done a really good job of deploying capital, which is a testament to their leadership," said Gary Cooper, an analyst with Bank of America Securities. "They've done a great job of spending the money they needed to in order to have state-of-the-art production in assembly facilities with excess capacity, but they haven't overspent."[116]

The ability to respond quickly to new developments was another hallmark of Polaris's success. "They're very flexible, very agile," said Cooper. "They have a flexible production line both in Roseau and Spirit Lake, and that allows them to be a lot more nimble than other companies. So when there are dislocations or flat demand in any market, they adapt pretty quickly."[117]

Polaris demonstrated that trademark agility in numerous ways. By designing products to be simpler to manufacture, designing and building its own engines, and continually improving production processes, Polaris was able to produce a better product at lower cost than its competitors.

In its drive toward industry-leading quality, Polaris continued to invest in Roseau, "where the heart and soul of Polaris was born," said Tiller. A new 58,000-square-foot injection molding facility was completed in the summer of 1998. Then in 2002 the company augmented efficiency of its ATV and snowmobile production with a 68,000-square-foot expansion at the Roseau plant. With four new assembly lines, additional diagnostic and statistical process control equipment, and a redesigned welding department, Polaris managed to improve quality, flexibility, and throughput—all in one fell swoop. That fall, the company also began expanding its engineering capabilities in Roseau with a new $7 million facility and announced plans for a 33,000-square-foot addition to the ATV production facility in Spirit Lake, Iowa.

And, of course, Polaris would continue its focus on innovation and diversity, offering "The Way Out" for every season, region, and lifestyle. As Richard Edwards, director of investor relations, observed, "New products are the lifeblood of the company. Historically, Polaris has always been an innovative company, but Tom [Tiller] has brought a number of new managers on board who are even more focused on new product development and getting the product right the first time."[118]

No longer would Polaris settle for beating the local competition or being better than it had been the year before. Now its goal was to be number one in the industry—in all aspects of the industry, including quality of product, support of its approximately 2,000 dealers, and service to customers. Polaris was committed to providing a superior riding experience by offering top-quality products, hassle-free shopping experiences, superior service and support, improved financing, and fun, stylish accessories.

As Tom Tiller proudly proclaimed, "We firmly believe the best lies ahead for Polaris."[119]

NOTES TO SOURCES

Chapter One

1. Edgar Hetteen and Jay Lemke, *Breaking Trail* (Bemidji: Focus Publishing, 1998), p. 52.
2. Edgar Hetteen, interview by Jeffrey L. Rodengen, recording, 21 May 2002, Write Stuff Enterprises.
3. Hetteen and Lemke, *Breaking Trail*, 56.
4. Ibid, 62.
5. Ibid, 64.
6. Ibid, 66.
7. Ibid, 67.
8. Ibid, 68.
9. David Johnson, "A Hometown Heritage: Three Keys to the Success of the Company, Polaris Industries, Inc." (Student paper, St. John's University, 1999), p.10.
10. Jerry Bassett, *Polaris Pioneers* (St. Paul: Recreational Publications, 1989), p.10.
11. Hetteen and Lemke, *Breaking Trail*, 60.
12. Johnson, "A Hometown Heritage," 10.
13. Hetteen and Lemke, *Breaking Trail*, 70.
14. Ibid; information provided by Edgar Hetteen to the authors, 3 September 2002.
15. "Sprayers Are Made by Firm in Roseau," *Roseau Times-Region*, 24 March 1949, 1.
16. Paul Knochenmus, interview by Jeffrey L. Rodengen, recording, 22 May 2002, Write Stuff Enterprises.
17. "Local Firm Reaches Nationwide Market with Hometown Product," *Roseau Times-Region*, 26 April 1951, 1.
18. "Hetteen Hoist Product Accepted As Regular in MM Equipment," *Roseau Times-Region*, 28 January 1954, 1.
19. "Polaris Industries to Remain at Roseau," *Roseau Times-Region*, 15 April 1954, 1.
20. "Polaris Industries to Expand; New Building to Start Immediately," *Roseau Times-Region*, 20 October 1955, 1.
21. David Johnson, interview by Jeffrey L. Rodengen, recording, 22 May 2002, Write Stuff Enterprises.
22. Knochenmus, interview.
23. Michael Dapper, *Illustrated Polaris Snowmobile Buyer's Guide* (Osceola: Motorbooks International, 1993), 10; Bassett, *Polaris Pioneers*, 16–17.
24. Knochenmus, interview.
25. Ibid.
26. Hetteen and Lemke, *Breaking Trail*, 100.
27. Ibid, 101.
28. David Johnson, interview.
29. Mitchell Johnson, "History of Polaris Industries, Roseau Minnesota," *County of Roseau Centennial, 1895–1995*, 265.
30. Dapper, *Illustrated Polaris Guide*, 11.
31. Bassett, *Polaris Pioneers*, 21.
32. *Roseau Times-Region*, 17 May 1956.
33. Dapper, *Illustrated Polaris Guide*, 11.

Chapter Two

1. Bassett, *Polaris Pioneers*, 23.
2. Hetteen and Lemke, *Breaking Trail*, 105.
3. Ibid.
4. Ibid, 108.
5. Ibid, 106.
6. Hetteen, interview; Hetteen and Lemke, *Breaking Trail*, 106.
7. Hetteen and Lemke, *Breaking Trail*, 106.
8. Ibid, 109.
9. Ibid, 113.
10. Hetteen, interview.
11. *Bemidji Daily Pioneer*, 2 February 1957, 6.
12. "Roseau Product Gets Recognition," *Roseau Times-Region*, 7 February 1957, 1.
13. Bassett, *Polaris Pioneers*, 39.
14. *Roseau Times-Region*, 26 September 1957.
15. "Sno-Traveler to Be Tested in Army Show," *Roseau Times-Region*, 23 January 1958, 3.
16. "Sno-Traveler Successful at Snow Show," *Roseau Times-Region*, 30 January 1958, 1.
17. Johnson, "History of Polaris Industries," 266.
18. Bassett, *Polaris Pioneers*, 25.
19. Ibid.
20. "Polaris Sno-Traveler Sales Invading Widespread Area," *Roseau Times-Region*, 11 December 1958, 1.
21. Bassett, *Polaris Pioneers*, 36.
22. "Polaris Sales Top Previous Years," *Roseau Times-Region*, 21 May 1959, 1.
23. Hetteen and Lemke, *Breaking Trail*, 4.
24. Ibid, 4.
25. Ibid, 5.
26. Knochenmus, interview.
27. Hetteen, interview.
28. Bessie Billberg, interview by Jeffrey L. Rodengen, recording, 22 May 2002, Write Stuff Enterprises.
29. Rudy Billberg, interview by Jeffrey L. Rodengen, recording, 22 May 2002, Write Stuff Enterprises.
30. Bassett, *Polaris Pioneers*, 42.
31. Ibid, 43.
32. "End 1,200 Mile Sno-Traveler Trip thru Alaskan Wilds," *Roseau Times-Region*, 31 March 1960, 1.
33. "Sno-Traveler to South Pole; Yearly Production Doubles," *Roseau Times-Region*, 21 January 1960, 1.

Chapter Two Sidebar: Staying Afloat

1. Polaris Industries, Inc., sales document, 1960, 4.
2. David Johnson, interview.
3. Polaris sales document, 7.

Chapter Two Sidebar: Sno-Traveler Line

1. Dapper, *Illustrated Polaris Guide*, 24.

Chapter Three

1. Hetteen and Lemke, *Breaking Trail*, 143.
2. Ibid, 144.
3. Bassett, *Polaris Pioneers*, 50.
4. Hetteen and Lemke, *Breaking Trail*, 145.
5. Ibid, 145.
6. Information provided by Edgar Hetteen to the authors, 3 September 2002.
7. Hetteen and Lemke, *Breaking Trail*, 147.
8. Ibid.
9. "Polaris Reorganizes; Plans Stock Sales," *Roseau Times-Region*, 7 July 1960, p. 1.
10. Lloyd Fugleberg, interview by Jeffrey L. Rodengen, recording, 22 May 2002, Write Stuff Enterprises.
11. Marlys Brandt, interview by Richard F. Hubbard, recording, 21 May 2002, Write Stuff Enterprises.
12. Bob Granitz, interview by Richard F. Hubbard, recording, 21 May 2002, Write Stuff Enterprises.
13. Bassett, *Polaris Pioneers*, 51.
14. Polaris Industries, Inc., Report of Audit, March 1964.
15. Ibid.
16. "Polaris Aims At Increase; Elects Nine," *Roseau Times-Region*, 31 May 1961, 1.
17. "Polaris Industries Experiments with Fiberglass on Travelers," *Roseau Times-Region*, 28 December 1961, 1.
18. Bassett, *Polaris Pioneers*, 59.
19. "Polaris Now in New Building," *Roseau Times-Region*, 2 May 1963, 1.
20. Ibid.
21. Bob Eastman, interview by Jeffrey L. Rodengen, recording, 21 May 2002, Write Stuff Enterprises.

22. "Polaris in New Building," 1.
23. "Sno-Travelers Proved Best," *Roseau Times-Region,* 2 March 1961, 1.
24. Bassett, *Polaris Pioneers,* 54.
25. Ibid, 55.
26. Ibid, 60.
27. Ibid.
28. Jerry Bassett, *Polaris Partners* (St. Paul: Recreational Publications, 1994), 9.
29. Polaris Report of Audit, March 1964.
30. Allan Hetteen to Polaris shareholders, May 1964.
31. Mike Hetteen, interview by Richard F. Hubbard, recording, 21 May 2002, Write Stuff Enterprises.
32. Polaris Report of Audit, March 1964.
33. Granitz, interview.

Chapter Three Sidebar: Hetteen's Adventure

1. Hetteen and Lemke, *Breaking Trail,* 172.

Chapter Three Sidebar: All for One

1. McNeil-Lehrer Essay, 35th Anniversary documentary, summer 1989.
2. Jerry Endrizzi, interview by Richard F. Hubbard, recording, 22 May 2002, Write Stuff Enterprises.
3. David Johnson, interview.
4. Ibid.
5. Knochenmus, interview.
6. Granitz, interview.
7. Fugleberg, interview.
8. Granitz, interview.

Chapter Four

1. Johnson, "History of Polaris Industries," 268.
2. "New Traveler Models Hilite Polaris Conference," *Roseau Times-Region,* 2 July 1964, 1.
3. Jim Bernat, interview by Jeffrey L. Rodengen, recording, 22 May 2002, Write Stuff Enterprises.
4. Donald Hedlund, interview by Jeffrey L. Rodengen, recording, 21 May 2002, Write Stuff Enterprises.
5. "New Traveler Models," 1.
6. Bassett, *Polaris Pioneers,* 63.
7. Ibid, 69.
8. *Polaris Post,* February 1965, 3.
9. Bassett, *Polaris Pioneers,* 68.
10. Ibid.
11. "Polaris Distributors Sign Orders of $4,000,000," *Roseau Times-Region,* June 23, 1966, p. 1.
12. Ibid.
13. Jerry Montgomery, "'Iron Dogs' to Meet at Phalen," *St. Paul Pioneer Press,* 24 January 1965, 16.
14. *St. Paul Pioneer Press,* 31 January 1965, 1.

15. "First International Snow Vehicle Races Fascinating," *Roseau Times-Region,* 18 February 1965, 1.
16. "Mustangs Race to Victory," *Polaris Post,* March 1965, 1.
17. "Prize Winning Colt, with Trophies," *Polaris Post,* April 1966, 1.
18. "Polaris Machines Score Heavily in St. Paul Winter Carnival Contests," *Roseau Times-Region,* 3 February 1966, 1.
19. "Polaris Machines Sweep Races around Territory," *Roseau Times-Region,* 3 March 1966, 1.
20. "Hot Sport on Snow," *Business Week,* 28 January 1967, 137.
21. Bassett, *Polaris Pioneers,* 65.
22. Ibid, 71.
23. Montgomery, "'Iron Dogs,'" 16.
24. "The Shape of the Industry," *Snow-Goer,* September 1971, 11.
25. "Snowmobile Bounces into Acclaim and Protest," *New York Times,* 3 March 1968, V-7.
26. Leonard Sloane, "What's a Cross between Bobsled and Half-Track and Sells for $600–$1,700? Snowmobile," *New York Times,* 3 December 1967, III-1.
27. Bassett, *Polaris Pioneers,* 73.
28. "Polaris Industries Opens Traveler Plant in Canada," *Roseau Times-Region,* 19 August 1965, 1.
29. "Polaris Expanding Factory Building; Upholstery Plant," *Roseau Times-Region,* 22 September 1966, 1.
30. "Polaris Office Complex Remodeling Job Started," *Roseau Times-Region,* 6 July 1967, 1.
31. "Polaris Distributors Sign Orders of $4,000,000," *Roseau Times-Region,* 23 June 1966, 1.
32. Jerry Shank, interview by Richard F. Hubbard, recording, 22 May 2002, Write Stuff Enterprises.
33. Ibid.
34. Ibid.
35. Ibid.
36. Mitchell Johnson, interview by Richard F. Hubbard, recording, 12 August 2002, Write Stuff Enterprises.
37. Bassett, *Polaris Pioneers,* 87–89.
38. Shank, interview.
39. Polaris Report of Audit, March 1964.
40. Touche, Ross, Bailey & Smart, Polaris Industries, Inc., Purchase by Textron Inc., 1968 (Audit), 12.
41. "The Shape of the Industry," *Snow-Goer,* September 1971, 11.
42. Johnson, "History of Polaris Industries," 268.

Chapter Four Sidebar: Coast-to-Coast Colts

1. Frank Sleeper, "Cops, Dogs and Snowmobiles without Snow," *Sports Illustrated,* 9 January 1967, 52.

2. "Men on Mustangs End Record-Breaking Trek," *Roseau Times-Region,* 29 December 1966, 1.
3. Ibid.

Chapter Five

1. Bassett, *Polaris Pioneers,* 82.
2. Mike Hetteen, interview.
3. Ibid.
4. "Polaris Stockholders to Vote July 31 on Sale Of Roseau Firm to Textron," *Roseau Times-Region,* 25 July 1968, 1.
5. Ibid.
6. "Polaris Building Addition to Factory; Expect to Up Production by 75 Per Cent," *Roseau Times-Region,* 15 February 1968, 1.
7. "Polaris Producing; Payroll Now 500," *Roseau Times-Region,* 29 August 1968, 1.
8. Bill Vint, *Warriors of Winter* (Milwaukee: Market Communications, 1977), 93.
9. Ibid, 114.
10. Clayton Carlson, interview by Richard F. Hubbard, recording, 21 May 2002, Write Stuff Enterprises.
11. Vint, *Warriors of Winter,* 96.
12. "Polaris Thrill Show Tops with Bonanza's Big Stars," *Roseau Times-Region,* 13 February 1969, 1.
13. "Polaris Expanding; Sets Goals for Year Ahead," *Roseau Times-Region,* 3 July 1969, 1.
14. "Polaris Completing Major Expansion; Payroll Total Is 997 in Roseau Factory," *Roseau Times-Region,* 27 November 1969, 1.
15. Vint, *Warriors of Winter,* 104.
16. "Wahlberg Gen. Manager Polaris Roseau Operations," *Roseau Times-Region,* 12 February 1970, 1.
17. "Polaris Expanding," 1.
18. Lee S. Isgur, "Snowmobiles on Wall Street," *Snow Goer Trade,* October 1971, 30.
19. "Snow Job?" *Forbes,* 1 February 1970, 35.
20. "Polaris Completing Major Expansion," 1.
21. "Allan Hetteen Retires As President of Polaris Industries June 1," *Roseau Times-Region,* 28 May 1970, 1
22. "Specialize Polaris Top Team for Long Term Growth Aims," *Roseau Times-Region,* 7 October 1971, 1.
23. "Polaris Seeks Diversification, Strength Here," *Roseau Times-Region,* 5 November 1970, 1.
24. Ibid.
25. Isgur, "Snowmobiles on Wall Street," 30.
26. "Polaris Seeks Diversification," 1.

27. John T. Prusak, "Industry Sales: Through the Years," *Snowmobile Business,* September 1996, 86.
28. "Snowmobile Sales Hit the Skids," *Business Week,* 13 March 1971, 134.

Chapter Five Sidebar: Bonanza

1. Bassett, *Polaris Pioneers,* 79.

Chapter Five Sidebar: Safety and Noise

1. "Snowmobile Bounces," V-7.
2. "Polaris Announces Safety Program; Quieter Machines," *Roseau Times-Region,* 17 October 1968, 6.
3. Clifford Simak, "Industry Is Making Snowmobiles Safer," *Minneapolis Tribune,* 4 February 1973, 19A.
4. "Sound Engineering: What's It All About?" *PolariScope,* July 1974, p. 1.

Chapter Six

1. "Future Is Promising for Polaris, Roseau Businessmen Are Told," *Roseau Times-Region,* 4 November 1971, 1.
2. "Specialize Polaris Top Team," 1.
3. "Polaris Sales Boosted by 60 Per Cent in Past Year," *Roseau Times-Region,* 10 February 1972, 1.
4. Prusak, "Industry Sales," 82.
5. "The Year of the Crunch for Snowmobiles," *Business Week,* 27 January 1973, 75.
6. "Sears May Quit Selling Snowmobiles, Aide Says," *Minneapolis Star,* 30 March 1972, B16.
7. "Agreement between Polaris, Union Set; Wages, Benefits for Three Year Period," *Roseau Times-Region,* 22 June 1972, 1.
8. "Polaris Starts Production on New Introduced Models," *Roseau Times-Region,* 23 March 1972, 8.
9. "Polaris Expansion Project Begins Here," *Roseau Times-Region,* 5 October 1972, 1.
10. "Polaris Leaders Emphasize Strong Future for Company," *Roseau Times-Region,* 21 December 1972, 1.
11. "Polaris Production Run Ended," *Roseau Times-Region,* 7 December 1972, 1.
12. Robert J. Hagen, "Snowmobiling Runs Out of Gas," *Minneapolis Tribune,* 17 March 1974, C13.
13. Herbert C. Graves to Allan Hetteen, 11 January 1973.
14. "The Year of the Crunch," 75.
15. Jim Fuller, "Snowmobile Business Growth Halted, But More Stable Expansion Expected," *Minneapolis Tribune,* 21 January 1973, C15.

16. Ralph Thornton, "Snowmobiling... Darker Days Ahead?" *Minneapolis Star,* 29 November 1973, 1C.
17. Hagen, "Snowmobiling Runs Out of Gas," C13.
18. "Polaris Management Cutback Announced," *Roseau Times-Region,* 24 January 1974, 1.
19. "Polaris Begins '75 Production," *Roseau Times-Region,* 18 April 1974, 1.
20. Chuck Baxter, interview by Jeffrey L. Rodengen, recording, 21 May 2002, Write Stuff Enterprises.
21. "Fuchs Explains Polaris Goal of Full-Time Work in Roseau," *Roseau Times-Region,* 21 November 1974, 1.
22. Prusak, "Industry Sales," 82.
23. "Polaris Begins Production; Expect $4,000,000 Payroll," *Roseau Times-Region,* 3 April 1975, 1.
24. "Snowmobile Makers Melt Away As a Lean Year Takes Its Toll," *Wall Street Journal,* 24 April 1975, 1.
25. "Polaris President Forecasts Growth of Roseau Facility," *Roseau Times-Region,* 21 November 1974, 1.
26. "Polaris Begins Production," 1.
27. Prusak, "Industry Sales," 82.
28. "Production Picks Up at Polaris Plant," *Roseau Times-Region,* 13 May 1976, 1.
29. "A Smoother Trail for Snowmobile Makers," *Business Week,* 13 December 1976, 60.
30. Robert J. Hagen, "Snowmobile Makers Expect Profits," *Minneapolis Tribune,* 1 August 1976, 15C.
31. "Production Picks Up at Polaris Plant," 1.
32. "Polaris Hall of Fame," *Polaris Spirit,* Spring 1986, 6.
33. Shank, interview.
34. Prusak, "Industry Sales," 82.
35. "Polaris President Calls Company Outlook Good," *Roseau Times-Region,* 3 November 1977, 1.
36. Prusak, "Industry Sales," 82.
37. Ellen Wojahn, "Tough Sledding," *Minnesota Corporate Report,* January 1982, 64.
38. Eastman, interview.
39. "Polaris IFS Technology Pays Off in 1980 TX-L Indy," *Roseau Times-Region,* 29 November 1979, 19.
40. "Polaris People Cut As Production Drops," *Roseau Times-Region,* 7 February 1980, 1.
41. Pam Hetteen, interview by Richard F. Hubbard, recording, 22 May 2002, Write Stuff Enterprises.
42. Ken Wojciehowski, interview by Jeffrey L. Rodengen, recording, 22 May 2002, Write Stuff Enterprises.
43. Arnold Ochs, interview by Richard F. Hubbard, recording, 24 July 2002, Write Stuff Enterprises.
44. "New Polaris President Has Polaris Service, Optimism,"

Roseau Times-Region, 14 February 1980, p. 1.
45. David Johnson, interview.
46. Wojahn, "Tough Sledding," 66.
47. "Polaris Confident Despite 4-Week Cut in Production," *Roseau Times-Region,* 10 July 1980, 1.
48. Mary Zins, interview by Richard F. Hubbard, recording, 31 January 2001, Write Stuff Enterprises.
49. "Textron-Bombardier Talk Sale of Polaris; Negotiations Continuing," *Roseau Times-Region,* 4 September 1980, 1.
50. "Proposed Deal Will Help Both Companies, Bombardier Exec Says," *Snow Goer Trade,* October 1980, 5.
51. Zins, interview.
52. "Polaris Purchase Dies; Opposition," *Roseau Times-Region,* 30 October 1980, 1.
53. "Polaris Snowmobile Build Cut-Back 'Exactly That,'" *Roseau Times-Region,* 22 January 1981, 1.

Chapter Six Sidebar: In Memory

1. "Allan Hetteen Killed As Tractor Overturns," *Roseau Times-Region,* 29 November 1973, 1.

Chapter Six Sidebar: Death in Racing Family

1. Bassett, *Polaris Pioneers,* 128.
2. Eastman, interview.
3. Keith Hansen, "Polaris, Yamaha, IFSA Out Arctic Cat, Bombardier In," *Snow Goer Trade,* June/July 1978, 5.

Chapter Seven

1. "Bankers Visit Polaris for Check of Plant Facilities," *Roseau Times-Region,* 25 March 1981, 1.
2. Bassett, *Polaris Pioneers,* 136.
3. Fugleberg, interview.
4. David Dokken, interview by Richard F. Hubbard, recording, 30 July 2002, Write Stuff Enterprises.
5. Bassett, *Polaris Partners,* 17.
6. Baxter, interview.
7. "Production Run Ends," *Headlines Between Deadlines,* Spring 1981, 1.
8. "Polaris Is Sold to Management Group," *Roseau Times-Region,* 22 July 1981, 1.
9. Wojahn, "Tough Sledding," 66.
10. Hall Wendel, Jr., interview by Jeffrey L. Rodengen, recording, 6 August 2002, Write Stuff Enterprises.
11. Ibid.
12. Ibid.
13. Ibid.
14. Fugleberg, interview.
15. Wayne Hanson, "Polaris Declares Independence." *Snow Goer Trade,* August/September 1981, 8.

16. Zins, interview.
17. Udell Nelson, interview by Richard F. Hubbard, recording, 27 June 2002, Write Stuff Enterprises.
18. Robert Moe, interview by Richard F. Hubbard, recording, 24 September 2002, Write Stuff Enterprises.
19. "Polaris Is Sold to Management Group," 1.
20. Hanson, "Polaris Declares Independence," 8.
21. Zins, interview.
22. Granitz, interview.
23. Fugleberg, interview.
24. "Polaris to Make Clutches for E-Z-Go Starting Soon," *Roseau Times-Region,* 12 August 1981, 1.
25. Bassett, *Polaris Partners,* 42–43.
26. Baxter, interview.
27. Ibid.
28. Robert Nygaard, interview by Richard F. Hubbard, recording, 31 January 2002, Write Stuff Enterprises.
29. Bassett, *Polaris Partners,* 44.
30. Wojahn, "Tough Sledding," 66.
31. "Polaris Cuts Off Talks on Arctic Acquisition," *Roseau Times-Region,* 10 February 1982, 1
32. Baxter, interview.
33. "Polaris Prepares for June 1 Build; Plans New Department," *Roseau Times-Region,* 7 April 1982, 1.
34. "Polaris Officials Expect Good Year—New Products Soon," *Roseau Times-Region,* 9 June 1982, 1.
35. "Polaris Distributes $200,000 Bonus; Pays Up Debts," *Roseau Times-Region,* 15 December 1982, 1.
36. Nygaard, interview, 31 January 2002.
37. Zins, interview.
38. "Polaris Officials Expect Good Year," 1.
39. "Polaris Birthday Marked by 375 People on 'Build," *Roseau Times-Region,* 2 June 1982, 1.
40. Bassett, *Polaris Partners,* 20.
41. Baxter, interview.
42. Ed Skomoroh, interview by Richard F. Hubbard, recording, 31 January 2002, Write Stuff Enterprises.
43. Bassett, *Polaris Partners,* 27.
44. "Polaris Distributes $200,000 Bonus," 1.
45. Nygaard, interview, 31 January 2002.
46. Robert Nygaard, interview by Melody Maysonet, recording, 15 October 2002, Write Stuff Enterprises.
47. Ed Skomoroh, interview by Melody Maysonet, recording, 17 October 2002, Write Stuff Enterprises.
48. Ibid.
49. Skomoroh, interview, 30 January 2002.
50. Wanda Campbell, interview by Richard F. Hubbard, recording, 30 January 2002, Write Stuff Enterprises.
51. "Figures Help Tell the Story," *Polaris Insights,* April 1983, 1.

Chapter Seven Sidebar:
Employee Relations

1. "Polaris Employees May Vote on Union Decertification; Election Set for July 1," *Roseau Times-Region,* 17 March 1982.
2. "Polaris Ends Good Run; Profit Sharing in Future," *Roseau Times-Region,* 22 September 1982, 1.
3. Zins, interview.
4. Bassett, *Polaris Partners,* 75.

Chapter Eight

1. "Polaris Production Begins to Roll Here," *Roseau Times-Region,* 1 June 1983, 1.
2. Mike Malone, interview by Jeffrey L. Rodengen, recording, 31 January 2002, Write Stuff Enterprises.
3. Ibid.
4. Polaris press release, 27 February 1984.
5. Bassett, *Polaris Partners,* 25.
6. "'Very, Very Bright Future' Affirms President of Growth Oriented Polaris," *Roseau Times-Region,* 18 July 1984, 11.
7. Baxter, interview.
8. Ibid.
9. Dean Hedlund, interview by Jeffrey L. Rodengen, recording, 9 July 2002, Write Stuff Enterprises.
10. Skomoroh, interview, 17 October 2002.
11. "'Very, Very Bright Future,'" 11.
12. "Polaris Wraps Up Production Year, Looks to '85 with New Products," *Roseau Times-Region,* 28 November 1984, 1.
13. Jan Dutcher, "Polaris Employees Gather for Distribution of $452,000," *Roseau Times-Region,* 19 December 1984, 1.
14. Jan Dutcher, "Governor Rides Polaris All-Terrain Vehicle," *Roseau Times-Region,* 27 March 1985, 1.
15. David Mona, interview by Jeffrey L. Rodengen, recording, 10 July 2002, Write Stuff Enterprises.
16. Ibid.
17. Bassett, *Polaris Partners,* 48.
18. Endrizzi, interview.
19. Jan Dutcher, "Full Production of Polaris ATVs Continues," *Roseau Times-Region,* 21 August 1985, 1
20. Bennett Morgan, interview by Jeffrey L. Rodengen, recording, 30 January 2002, Write Stuff Enterprises.
21. Sharon Warren Walsh, "ATV Settlement Provides for Rider Training Programs," *Washington Post,* 15 March 1988, C3.
22. Neal St. Anthony, "Polaris Managers Dig Out of Avalanche,"

Minneapolis Star-Tribune, 5 November 1989, 1D.
23. Jan Dutcher, "Polaris Employees Gather for $620,000 Profit Distribution," *Roseau Times-Region,* 18 December 1985, 1.
24. Pam Hetteen, interview.
25. Moe, interview.
26. "Polaris Files for Public Offering," *Snowmobile Business,* December 1986, 12.
27. Jan Dutcher, "Polaris Employees Gather for $885,000 Profit Distribution," *Roseau Times-Region,* 17 December 1986, 1.
28. Neal St. Anthony, "Polaris Managers Dig Out of Avalanche," *Minneapolis Star-Tribune,* 5 November 1989, 1D.
29. Jan Dutcher, "Polaris Holds Awareness Meeting," *Roseau Times-Region,* 23 September 1987, 1.
30. Dutcher, "Polaris Employees Gather for $620,000 Profit Distribution," 1.
31. "Polaris Announces Plant Expansion," *Snowmobile Business,* September 1986, 12.
32. Jan Dutcher, "Polaris Starts Production in New Plant Addition," *Roseau Times-Region,* 6 May 1987, 12.
33. Nygaard, interview, 31 January 2002.
34. Bassett, *Polaris Partners,* 77.
35. Correspondence from Ed Skomoroh to Melody Maysonet, 11 November 2002.
36. Marlys Olsen, interview by Jeffrey L. Rodengen, recording, 22 May 2002, Write Stuff Enterprises.
37. Jeff Bjorkman, interview by Jeffrey L. Rodengen, recording, 30 January 2002, Write Stuff Enterprises.
38. Dave Mowitz, "Utility Vehicles: Buyers Guide," *Successful Farming,* November 1998.
39. Correspondence from Ed Skomoroh, 11 November 2002.
40. Candace Schneider, "6 x 6 ATV Used by Military Spy Body," *Roseau Times-Region,* 2 January 1991, 1.
41. John Harris, "Noisemakers," *Forbes,* 29 October 1990, 104.
42. Correspondence from Ed Skomoroh, 11 November 2002.
43. Gordon Black, "Inside Polaris: Success against the Odds," *Dealernews,* November 1989, 107.
44. Injection Research Specialists, Inc. v. Polaris Industries, L.P., 1998, WL 536585 (Fed. Cir. Colo.), 13 August 1998; Polaris Industries Inc. 1998 Annual Report, 24.
45. Bassett, *Polaris Partners,* 30.
46. Ibid, 31.
47. Candace Schneider, "Polaris Finishes Year of Expansion," *Roseau Times-Region,* 2 January 1991, 1.

48. Bassett, *Polaris Partners,* 31.
49. Nygaard, interview, 31 January 2002.
50. Ibid.
51. Polaris Industries Inc. Production History: 1970–2001, 70.
52. Nygaard, interview, 31 January 2002.
53. Nygaard, interview, 25 November 2002.
54. Bassett, *Polaris Partners,* 53.
55. Harris, "Noisemakers," 104.
56. "Polaris Will Distribute $1,428,635 for 1988," *Roseau Times-Region,* 14 December 1988, 1.
57. Duane Mattson, "Roseau C & C Association Gets Challenges and Cheer," *Roseau Times-Region,* 24 January 1990, 1.
58. Baxter, interview.
59. Ibid.
60. Polaris press release, 26 September 1991.
61. Nygaard, interview, 31 January 2002.
62. Bassett, *Polaris Partners,* 56.
63. "Polaris Takes to the Water," *Roseau Times-Region,* 6 August 1991, 1.
64. Bassett, *Polaris Partners,* 59.
65. Michael Fibison, "Watercraft Has Polaris Busy in Summer," *Rochester (MN) Post-Bulletin,* 3 May 1993, 10.
66. Baxter, interview.

Chapter Eight Sidebar: Hetteen Returns

1. "Polaris Announces the Appointment of Edgar Hetteen to the Post of Company Spokesman," *Polaris Insights,* January 1984, 1.

Chapter Eight Sidebar: Johnson Retires

1. Jan Dutcher, "Polaris Co-founder, David Johnson, Retires after 42 years," *Roseau Times-Region,* 24 February 1988, 1.

Chapter Nine

1. "What a Party!" *Roseau Times-Region,* 5 August 1994, 1.
2. "The Mayor's Thoughts on Polaris," *Roseau Times-Region,* 22 July 1994, 1.
3. Dick Melvin, "Polaris Expands to New Iowa Plant," *Roseau Times-Region,* 24 June 1994, 1.
4. Dick Melvin, "Roseau Must Seek Growth," *Roseau Times-Region,* 24 June 1994, 4.
5. Dick Melvin, "The Roseau Double Standard," *Roseau Times-Region,* (undated).
6. "Susan E. Peterson, "Polaris Industries Will Soon Move Some Operations to Spirit Lake, Iowa," *Minneapolis Star-Tribune,* 25 June 1994, 18D.

7. Chuck Crone, interview by Jeffrey L. Rodengen, recording, 30 January 2002, Write Stuff Enterprises.
8. LaRae Krahn, interview by Jeffrey L. Rodengen, recording, 21 May 2002, Write Stuff Enterprises.
9. Crone, interview.
10. "Polaris Plant Opening," *Snowmobile Business,* February 1995, 8.
11. Polaris press release, 22 December 1994.
12. Polaris press release, 4 February 1995.
13. Polaris press release, 3 August 1995.
14. Polaris press release, 2 October 1995.
15. Martin Heinrich, interview by Richard F. Hubbard, recording, 1 July 2002, Write Stuff Enterprises.
16. Bjorkman, interview.
17. Heinrich, interview.
18. Ibid.
19. Ibid.
20. Bjorkman, interview.
21. "Polaris Plans to Build Engines at Osceola, Wisconsin Plant," *Snowmobile Business,* December 1995, 8.
22. "Polaris Warehousing to Move to South Dakota," *Snowmobile Business,* August 1996, 12.
23. Morgan, interview.
24. "Susan E. Peterson, "Polaris Industries Will Soon Move Some Operations to Spirit Lake, Iowa," *Minneapolis Star-Tribune,* 25 June 1994, 18D.
25. Hall Wendel, Jr., interview by Richard F. Hubbard, recording, 26 November 2002, Write Stuff Enterprises.
26. Marlys Knutson, interview by Richard F. Hubbard, recording, 13 January 2003, Write Stuff Enterprises.
27. Wendel, interview, 26 November 2002.
28. Correspondence from Ed Skomoroh, 11 November 2002.
29. Wendel, interview, 26 November 2002.
30. Correspondence from Ed Skomoroh, 11 November 2002.
31. "The Success of the Community Featured at the Roseau Civic and Commerce Banquet," *Roseau Times-Region,* 19 January 1996, 1.
32. Knutson, interview.
33. Polaris Industries Inc., 1996 Annual Report.
34. "Polaris Reorganizes into Business Units," *Snowmobile Business,* August 1996, 8.
35. Kevin Mollet, interview by Richard F. Hubbard, recording, 30 January 2002, Write Stuff Enterprises.
36. Polaris press release, 17 October 1996.

37. Polaris 1996 Annual Report, 9.

Chapter Ten

1. Polaris 1998 Annual Report, 29.
2. Paul Klebnikov, "Clear the Roads, Here Comes Victory," *Forbes,* 20 October 1997, 162.
3. Michael Dapper and Lee Klancher, *The Victory Motorcycle: The Making of a New American Motorcycle* (Osceola: MBI Publishing, 1998), 12.
4. Ibid.
5. Ibid, 15; Baxter, interview.
6. Klebnikov, "Clear the Roads," 162.
7. Tony Kennedy, "Polaris Revs Up for Motorcycles," *Minneapolis Star-Tribune,* 20 February 1997, 1D.
8. Tony Kennedy, "Polaris Rolls Out Its Motorcycle," *Minneapolis Star-Tribune,* 10 July 1998, 1D.
9. Mona, interview.
10. Polaris press release, 7 April 1998.
11. Susan E. Peterson, "GE Exec Is Named New Polaris President, CEO," *Minneapolis Star-Tribune,* 8 April 1998, 3D.
12. Tom Tiller, interview by Jeffrey L. Rodengen, recording, 30 January 2002, Write Stuff Enterprises.
13. Richard Edwards, interview by Jeffrey L. Rodengen, recording, 10 July 2002, Write Stuff Enterprises.
14. Janet Klis, interview by Richard F. Hubbard, recording, 22 July 2002, Write Stuff Enterprises.
15. Tiller, interview.
16. John Corness, interview by Jeffrey L. Rodengen, recording, 30 January 2002, Write Stuff Enterprises.
17. Malone, interview.
18. Corness, interview.
19. Ibid.
20. Ibid.
21. Susan E. Peterson, "Revving Up Polaris," *Minneapolis Star-Tribune,* 18 May 1999, 1D.
22. Tiller, interview.
23. Ibid.
24. Ibid.
25. Polaris press release, 24 February 1999.
26. Tiller, interview.
27. Morgan, interview.
28. John Evan Frook, "Snowmobile Sales Rev Up with Online Custom Orders," *B to B,* 28 May 2001, 4.
29. Scott Swenson, interview by Richard F. Hubbard, recording, 30 January 2002, Write Stuff Enterprises.
30. Ibid.
31. Carla Solberg, "Tom Tiller: CEO of Polaris Industries Inc." *Corporate Report-Minnesota,* 1 September 1999, 8.
32. Polaris press release, 1 February 2000.
33. Richard Petty, interview by Jeffrey L. Rodengen,

recording, 21 August 2002, Write Stuff Enterprises.
34. Darcy Betlach, interview by Richard F. Hubbard, recording, 23 August 2002, Write Stuff Enterprises.
35. Kate MacArthur and Laura Petrecca, "Polaris Mobilizes $8 Million Print, TV Effort," *Advertising Age,* 28 August 2000, 12.
36. Ibid.
37. Polaris press release, April 13, 2000.
38. Correspondence from Ed Skomoroh, 11 November 2002.
39. Ibid.
40. Ibid.
41. Ibid.
42. Mitchell Johnson, interview.
43. Correspondence from Ed Skomoroh, 11 November 2002.
44. Polaris press release, February 28, 2000.
45. Mitchell Johnson, interview.
46. David Johnson, interview.
47. Skomoroh, interview, 30 January 2002.
48. Correspondence from Ed Skomoroh, 11 November 2002.
49. MacArthur and Petrecca, "Polaris Mobilizes $8 Million Print, TV Effort," 12.
50. Polaris Industries Inc, 1999 Annual report, 5.
51. Polaris press release, 12 April 1999.
52. Tiller, interview.
53. Knutson, interview.
54. *Roseau Times-Region,* 2 March 1998.
55. Morgan, interview.
56. "Polaris Announces Largest New Product Launch in Company History," Polaris press release, 1 August 2002.
57. Jerrod Kelley, *ATV Sport,* May 2003.
58. Robert Jette, *ATV Test Guide,* 2003.
59. Dee DePass, "Army Buys Hundreds of ATVs," *Scripps Howard News Service,* 28 March 2003.
60. Polaris Industries Inc. 2001 Annual Report, 2.
61. Ron Bills, interview by Jeffrey L. Rodengen, recording, 31 January 2002, Write Stuff Enterprises.
62. Bills, interview.
63. "Polaris Redefines Watercraft Industry with MSX—The New American Watercraft," Polaris press release, 5 August 2002.
64. "Polaris Watercraft Launches New Sport Boat Line," Polaris press release, 23 January 2003.
65. Polaris 1999 Annual Report, 10.
66. Mark Blackwell, interview by Jeffrey L. Rodengen, recording, 31 January 2002, Write Stuff Enterprises.

67. Gary Gray, interview by Richard F. Hubbard, recording, 25 July 2002, Write Stuff Enterprises.
68. Blackwell, interview.
69. Ibid.
70. Betlach, interview.
71. Blackwell, interview.
72. Malone, interview.
73. "Viva Las Vegas," *American Motorcyclist,* December 2002, 18.
74. Ibid, 18, 19.
75. "Victory Makes Good, a Cinderella Story," *Cycle World,* January 2003, 82.
76. Gray, interview.
77. Jeff Whaley, interview by Richard F. Hubbard, recording, 8 August 2002, Write Stuff Enterprises.
78. "Victory Makes Good, a Cinderella Story," 85.
79. Arlen Ness, interview by Richard F. Hubbard, recording, 23 July 2002, Write Stuff Enterprises.
80. Blackwell, interview.
81. Greg Hedlund, interview by Jeffrey L. Rodengen, recording, 21 May 2002, Write Stuff Enterprises.
82. "ATVs Help Armed Forces Climb Harsh Terrain in Search of the Enemy," Polaris press release, 5 June 2002.
83. Greg Hedlund, interview.
84. Dee DePass, "Army Buys Hundreds of ATVs," *Scripps Howard News Service,* 28 March 2003.
85. Carmen Kwong, interview by Richard F. Hubbard, recording, 30 January 2002, Write Stuff Enterprises.
86. Tom Ruschhaupt, interview by Richard F. Hubbard, recording, 30 January 2002, Write Stuff Enterprises.
87. Ruschhaupt, interview.
88. Whaley, interview.
89. Ben Blackmon, interview by Richard F. Hubbard, recording, 2 August 2002, Write Stuff Enterprises.
90. Bill Fisher, interview by Richard F. Hubbard, recording, 30 January 2002, Write Stuff Enterprises.
91. Judy Kulsrud, interview by Jeffrey L. Rodengen, recording, 30 January 2002, Write Stuff Enterprises.
92. Todd Dannenberg, interview by Richard F. Hubbard, recording, 31 January 2002, Write Stuff Enterprises.
93. Ibid.
94. Ruschhaupt, interview.
95. Swenson, interview.
96. Brad Dokken, "Polaris' New Center in Roseau Is an Experience," *Grand Forks Herald,* 23 December 2001.

97. Correspondence from Bruno Silikowski to Melody Maysonet, November 2002.
98. Ibid.
99. Bruno Silikowski, interview by Melody Maysonet, recording, 16 December 2002, Write Stuff Enterprises.
100. Correspondence from Bruno Silikowski, November 2002.
101. Silikowski, interview.
102. Krahn, interview.
103. Tiller, interview.
104. Tim Dejong, interview by Richard F. Hubbard, recording, 31 January 2002, Write Stuff Enterprises.
105. Brandt, interview.
106. Duane Osell, interview by Richard F. Hubbard, recording, 22 May 2002, Write Stuff Enterprises.
107. Olsen, interview.
108. Tiller, interview.
109. Edwards, interview.
110. Petty, interview.
111. Baxter, interview.
112. Robert Evans, interview by Richard F. Hubbard, recording, 2 August 2002, Write Stuff Enterprises.
113. Joseph T. Hallinan, "In Uncertain Time, Americans Resort to Expensive Toys," *Wall Street Journal,* 27 August 2002.
114. Ibid.
115. Joe Hovorka, interview by Richard F. Hubbard, recording, 2 August 2002, Write Stuff Enterprises.
116. Gary Cooper, interview by Richard F. Hubbard, recording, 5 August 2002, Write Stuff Enterprises.
117. Ibid.
118. Edwards, interview.
119. Polaris 2001 Annual Report.

Chapter Ten Sidebar: Workmobiles

1. "Polaris Announces Largest New Product Launch in Company History," Polaris press release, 1 August 2002.
2. "The Polaris Professional Series 4x4 and 6x6," Polaris press release, 21 March 2002.
3. "Polaris Gets Down to Business with New Professional Series," Polaris press release, 21 March 2002.

Chapter Ten Sidebar: Roseau Flood

1. Terry Collins, "Dike Gives Way in Roseau; River under Sharp Scrutiny As Crest Looms," *Minneapolis Star Tribune,* 12 June 2002.
2. Dean Hedlund, interview.
3. Deborah Caulfield Rybak, "Polaris CEO on the Scene Fighting the Flood," *Minneapolis Star Tribune,* 12 June 2002.
4. Ibid.

INDEX

Page numbers in italics indicate photographs.